An ACRE of ENGLAND

An ACRE of ENGLAND

L. J. MANNERS

Reproduced from the private
printing entitled

A Countryman Looks Back

Illustrated by the author

GRESHAM BOOKS
in association with
FOSTERS' BOOKSHOP, WOOTTON BASSETT
WILTSHIRE, ENGLAND

An ACRE of ENGLAND by L. J. Manners, illustrated by
the author.

ISBN 0 905418 06 9

Reprinted by photolitho from the author's private printing of
1973, with additional photographs.

1st Impression 1977
2nd Impression 1981

Published by Gresham Books Ltd.
Gresham Press
Old Woking
Surrey
England

L. J. Manners, 1977
Gift Book Promotions Ltd.

Printed by
Staples Printers St. Albans Ltd.
The Priory Press
St. Albans, Herts.

PHOTOGRAPHS

Front cover: Cherhill White Horse
by permission of the Wiltshire Archaeological and Natural
History Society.

Pictures of the Manners family and Minety
by permission of Mrs. Millicent A. Gegg.

Malmesbury and Cirencester
by permission of the Radio Times Hulton Picture Library.

PREFACE

WHEN I first read, in manuscript, Mr. Leonard Manners' delightful book, I was at once entranced by the beautiful pencil sketches by the author, as much as the text, which is full of rich country humour, and of characters the like of which cannot be met with now-a-days. In fact it caused me to neglect my library book for a whole weekend! A production of this calibre is most unusual from the pen (and pencil) of a man who left the village school on his thirteenth birthday, and, on his own admission, even so spent half his time in school, drawing!

Mr. Manners has led his long life on his family farm, apart from his War service, of which he also has tales to tell. He delights to tell how he enlisted in Malmesbury, and was actually 'sworn in' by Alderman Albert Adye, the father of Mr. Sydney Adye, over the grocer's shop.

I am very honoured to be asked to write a preface to this delightful book, and I hope that all its readers will enjoy it as much as I did.

MURIEL L. BEAK,
Cross Hayes,
Malmesbury

INTRODUCTION

AN ACRE OF ENGLAND is the sort of book that should be written but so rarely gets into print. This account of life in Minety, a village hovering between Wiltshire and Gloucestershire, perpetuates in print a life style which has now vanished but which is none the less worthy of recording. Minety has had an interesting history standing as it does on the borders of Bradon Forest and yet in the pastoral country of North Wiltshire. None of its history is more interesting than the period covered by Mr. Manners. The transition from horse and cart through early motor cycles, bought from a firm in Oxford, to motor cars and aeroplanes is faithfully traced. Though remote, Minety had connections with the outside world, and just as Garsdon a few miles away was connected with the Washington family so Minety was the home of the Penn family the founders of Pennsylvania. In addition to a full account of the local worthies, Minety farmers and the occupants of the larger houses in the village, there are accounts of the impact of the outside world on the parish. The arrival of evacuees during the 1939 war is one of these, and in Mr. Manners' case it led to a lifelong friendship. The expulsion of the 'Bruderhof' from Frankfurt in Germany and their settlement in Ashton Keynes was another; the memory of this strange and exotic sect still flourishes in the neighbourhood. Many other things of interest appear in this book, the first aeroplane to be seen in Minety, the start of Unigate at Wootton Bassett, accounts of the old Turnpike tolls and the early motor cars and cycles and even a visit to the T.T. in the Isle of Man. But perhaps the most interesting part of this book to future generations and more especially to sociologists will be Mr. Manners' account of his farming experiences and expenses under the heading 'A Living from the Land'. For this alone the book will be read for many years to come.

R. E. SANDELL, M.A., F.S.A., F.L.S.,
Hon. Librarian,
Wiltshire Archaeological and
Natural History Society

LIST OF ACKNOWLEDGEMENTS

Mrs. Millicent A. Gegg, who graciously assisted the editing
of this book.

Dr. T. R. Thomson, *Bradon Forest*.

Daphne Moore, *A Short History of the V.W.H. Hunt*.

Brigadier O. F. G. Hogg, C.B.E., F.S.A., F.R.Hist.S., *Further
Light on the Ancestry of William Penn*.

Fred. S. Thacker, *The Stripling Thames*.

Rev. F. H. Manley, M.A., *Wiltshire Notes and Queries*.

G. M. Trevelyan, *English Social History*.

Dr. B. L. Hodge.

Dr. Belt and Devizes Museum.

Mrs. E. M. Levinge.

Mr. Basil G. Rathbone, County Archivist.

Mr. John Scott, United Dairies (Wholesale) Ltd., Wootton
Bassett.

Mr. Gervas Huxley.

Mrs. Elspeth Huxley.

Mrs. C. A. Ward, Red Lodge.

Mr. Bob Daniels.

Miss M. Beak.

Mr. P. Hawkins.

Mr. Oliver Read.

Mrs. L. L. Slade, Penn's Lodge.

Mr. P. H. Thomas, Purton.

Mr. John Patrick Abbott, *Family Patterns*.

Mrs. Robert Ross Haines

and many others too numerous to mention, to whom I am
grateful for their valuable help.

MAP REFERENCES

Map references are taken from the one inch to the mile map of Swindon District, Sheet 157, published by the Director General at the Ordnance Survey Office, Southampton.

Nott Stone ...	SU.027887
Nath's Oak ...	SU.028916
Hoar Stone ...	ST.985989
Eastcourt Well	ST.975926
Watkin's Corner	SU.088901
Bucks Well ...	SU.009903
Minety Pike ...	SU.029904
Three Bridges ...	SU.044934
Gospel Oak Farm	SU.052888
Black Dog Bridge	SU.052899
Duchy Rag Pike	SU.052903
Eastcourt Pike ...	ST.977926
Grange Farm ...	SU.041925
Murcott Sign Post	ST.965916

CONTENTS

An ACRE of ENGLAND

Brothers and sisters at Minety.
L. J. Manners, back row,
centre.

Silver Street School, 1902.

The author, 1918.

The Moor Farm, 1924.

Malmesbury, the market cross and abbey.

Cirencester, the abbey and gatehouse.

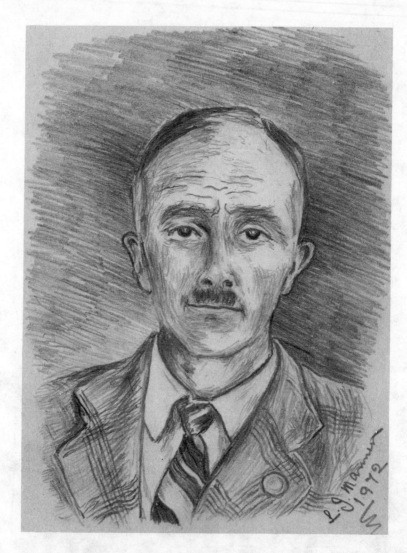

Self portrait by the Author.

CHAPTER ONE

How I came to look back

Introduction—John Ross

THE REASON I have written this book should really be explained as no doubt many will wonder why I, after practically a lifetime spent as a farmer, should at the age of seventy plus get down to the task of trying my hand at writing.

Now to give what was the final deciding factor we have to go back to the late nineteen-thirties and the second World War. Hostile aircraft were dropping high explosive and incendiary bombs on towns and cities and as a result, to save lives, many women and children, and in fact any who were not vitally needed to remain behind, were evacuated to the rural areas to be taken in by the local people—in some cases whole families.

Having a large house at the Moor Farm my wife agreed to take two families, a Mr. and Mrs. Alec Black and their daughter Irene, and a Mrs. Ross and her son John, twelve years of age, which was about the same age as my own son John. So as to know them apart we called the second John, Jack. Mrs. Ross was already widowed so I tried to make the boy happy and get him interested in farm life. He very soon came to enjoy giving me a hand and was helpful in many ways. Both boys were given five shillings a week pocket money. It wasn't long before Jack was helping to milk the cows and to make himself really useful.

Although I had a Fordson tractor I also had a couple of old cars which we stripped down and used for work on the land, especially in summer drawing haymaking machinery, etc. So Jack was soon driving a car, which of course was a big advantage to him later.

After the war he had the urge to return to London where he soon found employment as an acetylene welder, but by this time he was approaching the age of eighteen and was called up to do his period of National Service which he served with the Royal Engineers. By this time he had lost his mother and it was not long before he decided to take the plunge and take himself a wife. His fiancee was a London girl named Joan Wood who had also lost both her parents. As there was then an acute shortage of houses, knowing that often when working on a farm living accommodation is provided, Jack looked around and found a job with a cottage at Easton Grey, where he had charge of a herd of Guernseys. So the wedding was arranged to take place at Easton Grey. Jack asked me if I would "give the bride away" which I was only too pleased to do. My wife and I attended the wedding and the reception afterwards at Malmesbury.

Besides being ambitious, Jack was clever with his hands, a good artist and mechanic and he became particularly interested in sewing machines.

Coming back to this district he was in business in Cirencester for a time before moving to Swindon where he opened a shop in Market Street known as Swindon Sewing Machine Service. By dint of hard work and eye catching advertisements he soon had a thriving business and was able to open more shops. They now had two small children, Gillian and Martin, and it looked as though things were at last going his way.

About three years ago Jack brought his wife and children to visit us at Minety. I was laid up with a chill at the time. He brought the children upstairs to see me and asked if they could look upon us as their grandparents, having none of their

1

own, and if they could call me "Grandpa." We readily agreed and then Jack said he would like the children to hear some of my old stories, leaving a tape recorder so that when I felt fit enough I could sit up in bed and tell them and promising that when I recovered he would come with his car and take us to Swindon and shew us around and bring us home.

I was soon on the road to recovery, had used up the tape and asked Jack to bring another. This is where fate took a hand. The next I heard of poor Jack it was he who was ill, alas never to recover. My next visit to Swindon, instead of being his guests my wife and I were attending his funeral. He was only forty years of age with what seemed such a bright future before him and now in one "fell swoop" his children were fatherless and his wife a widow which shews how unpredictable life can be and hard as it is to bear these things they have to be accepted.

After I had used up the first tape I thought I would make some written notes for guidance and then it occurred to me that perhaps I could set some of the stories down in writing. So this is actually how I came to attempt the writing of this book.

* * * *

NOT ONLY was the year 1897 conspicuous as being the year of my birth, it was also the year of Queen Victoria's Golden Jubilee. Perhaps before getting into deeper water I should just say a few words about my family as this will make it easier for the reader to understand my attitude towards agricultural problems, etc. By far the greater part of my working life has been spent trying to wrest a living from the soil and I know only too well the frustrations of having to deal with an unsympathetic Government who have the power to fix the price of agricultural products while the Industrialists are free to charge what they themselves decide on so as to shew a good margin of profit for their shareholders. Added to this there is a seven-day working week and unpredictable weather conditions.

To get back to my story, my Grandfather, Edward Manners, came to Cooles Farm, Minety in about 1840 as a tenant farmer, married Mary Maundrell and brought up a family of six children, including Henry, my Father, who was born in 1853. For a time my father, whilst living at Cooles Farm, farmed the land opposite known as "Forty Acres" until 1887 when he took over Flistridge Farm, Minety, more of which will be written later.

My mother, Emma Jane, was a daughter of the late James Burgoyne, a schoolmaster from Devonshire. Many members of the family broke away from their hometown of Sidmouth to various parts of the country and my mother who also entered the teaching profession, whilst working as a pupil teacher at Wookey Hole met up with a teacher from Castle Eaton, who, on returning home to Wiltshire heard of a vacancy for a Headmistress at St. Leonard's School, Minety. She applied and was given the post. Her younger sister—later to become Mrs. Annie Catherine Lewis—soon joined her there, the two young single ladies taking up residence in the Schoolhouse adjoining the School. It was not long, however, before the local young farmers became regular attenders at the nearby St. Leonard's Church. My father, Henry Manners, at that time a member of the Church Choir, a foundation School Manager and later Vicar's Warden for many years, soon captured the heart of the young Headmistress.

Flistridge Farm, Minety, at that time occupied by my father, was then in the hands of the Trustees of the late Col. Perry-Keene of Minety House. The Tenancy Agreement, dated October 7th, 1887, which I still have in my possession, shows a yearly rental of £120. He often spoke of a terrible drought in the year 1893 that almost ended his farming career. The ground was as hard as concrete and the grass was so dry and brittle that with the swish of his walking-stick it snapped off like spikes of glass. They tore down branches from the trees to help feed the cattle. Many of his best cows had to be sold at £3-10-0 to £4-10-0 apiece as there was no grass and no hay for them.

2

Here I have details of a Sale conducted by Messrs. Moore & Hill (now Moore, Allen & Innocent) on July 15th, 1893.

Cattle prices from £12-15-0 best, down to £2.

17 Cattle realized	......	......	£100-12-6
13 Pigs realized	......	......	£33-16-0
45 Poultry realized	......	......	£3-11-6
			£138- 0-0

Charges: Advertisement in *Wilts. & Glos. Standard* and *North Wilts. Herald* and Bill Posting	....	......	£3-11-0
Commission	....	......	£3- 9-0
			£7- 0-0

TOTAL RAISED BY SALE	......	£138- 0-0
LESS CHARGES	....	£7- 0-0
BALANCE OF SALE	......	£131- 0-0

It is difficult to imagine how he survived, but I know he had a sideline or two such as Rate Collector and Assistant Overseer of the Poor which may have brought in some small income.

As there was no Master at the school and as always the usual number of unruly boys, the procedure was for the mistress to send a child with a note to the Vicarage, the Vicar forthwith bringing along his instrument of authority, which consisted of a sizeable stick duly exercised on the posterior of any offenders, peace reigning again for a time.

One elderly inhabitant of the village, Arthur Matthews, who lived at Little Tiddling Corner (now Upper Lyngrove) tells a good story about my father, who by that time knew his way to St. Leonard's pretty well, and was no doubt as regular an "attendant" as any of the children, except that his visits were after rather than during school hours. His story is that one day "Mr. Manners went up into Flist-ridge Wood and cut a gert stick as big as my thumb, brought en down to the school and said to your mother, 'Yer, thee cut this un into 'em. They won't want much o' that'!"

That's as far as that story goes, but one thing is certain, it was not long before there was a wedding and St. Leonard's School was again requiring a new Mistress. Being the first son I was, of course, christened Leonard. This is all so long ago that it is difficult to remember whether I was named after the Church or the Church named after me. As I do not claim to be a Saint we will consider that question settled.

* * * *

DURING my seventy-odd years I have turned my hand to many things with a limited amount of success, but in setting my hand to write this book I am venturing into the unknown as to the success or otherwise of my qualities as a writer. I must leave the verdict to those who have the patience to read it.

CHAPTER TWO

In and around Minety

Vale of White Horse

THERE seems to be many differences of opinion as to the area covered by the "Vale of White Horse." A hundred years ago it was shown on old maps as lying between the Thames and the Ock westward from Uffington but how far westward it is difficult to ascertain.

I have been to quite a lot of pains to satisfy myself and have come to the conclusion that the most ancient of the "White Horses" is the one at Uffington which is known to have existed for a thousand years. In Wiltshire it would appear that at various places between Swindon and Pewsey or within that vicinity there are evidences of at least eight "White Horses" so I shall not commit myself by attempting to give the exact area this covers. But at least I will say that it is possible it could include the whole of the area known at one time as "Bradon Forest."

Bradon Forest

MINETY was at one time almost in the centre of "Bradon Forest."

This was Royal Demesne and the favourite hunting ground of Royalty for many generations. The book *Braydon Forest* by Dr. T. R. Thomson covers its history for approximately a thousand years. Parts were disafforested and again reafforested by various kings during this time and finally disafforested in the reign of King Charles II. Portions of land or forest were bestowed or granted as favours and again seized and forfeited.

Bradon Forest in the reign of Henry III, approximately 15,000 acres.

After the reign of Charles II most of it came under private ownership and it was only during the reign of this monarch that to prove legal ownership it became necessary to hold written Title. Even under private ownership when most of the land became "estates" it still continually changed hands either for perhaps financial gain or sometimes because the owner could no longer afford to hold it.

This fine oak, on Nath's Farm, Minety, 28 feet in girth, is a survivor of Bradon Forest. Map ref. SU.028916.

Minety House

MINETY HOUSE is shown in Kelly's Directory for 1884 as being one of the chief Wiltshire country seats being at that time occupied by Colonel William Thomas Keene Perry-Keene, J.P., D.L., who was chief landowner and a magistrate for the County of Wilts. After his death in 1886-7 it was occupied by Henry Whatley Estridge until about 1900 when Tudor Lawrence Jones took up residence there, dying at the early age of 25 on January 17th, 1904. His parents had a stained glass window placed in the church to his memory.

Next came Major C. C. Gouldsmith, a great sportsman, cricket being one of his main interests, although he often turned out and played in goal for the village football team when we played in the "Fox Cover." Being a reservist, he was away with his regiment at the outbreak of hostilities in 1914 until the end of the war. After this he soon got things organised again.

5

Major Gouldsmith was, I believe, the first man in Minety to own a motor car and as his brother, Captain Jesse D. Gouldsmith, lived at Ashton Keynes House he was often to be seen driving back and forth. The roads then being of flint the car was followed in summer by a huge cloud of dust as high as the treetops and in winter everyone he happened to pass would be showered with mud and water. This became quite customary and no-one seemed to mind although you would be very unfortunate indeed if you met him on the Ashton Keynes turning from

Minety House.

the Lower Moor where, due to the ruts in the road and the high speed at which he took the corner, either dust, mud or water would be scattered in all directions.

Major Gouldsmith was also instrumental in forming a "Social Club," meetings being held on either one or two nights a week when he usually brought a couple of rabbits or a brace of birds as prizes for the shooting. The original Village Hall was opened by Mrs. Gouldsmith in 1930 although by that time they had left Minety and taken up residence in Cirencester.

He was a great one for organising entertainments in aid of local causes and delighted to appear on the stage at a concert. His party was named the "Minety Mountebanks." Major Gouldsmith's favourite piece was to come on the stage dressed as an old "rustic" with old hat, whiskers and smock, with a wisp of straw in his mouth and sing the old country song "I loves my Zarah." And there we must leave him for when the Gouldsmith family left Minety House Colonel Claude Kirby, another great theatrical genius, came there to live. By that time horses were playing a less important part with regard to transport and Colonel Kirby not being a hunting man, he converted the old saddle room over the garage and stabling into a workshop and playroom which was used for rehearsals by the local Dramatic Society which he ran.

One of the outstanding performances of Colonel Kirby took place at the Village Hall at a final rehearsal of one of his productions. We had all arrived at the hall when it was found that the caretaker had left the door locked and we were unable to get in. Being somewhat impetuous this was more than Colonel Kirby could stand. He was a strong man withal and clenching his fist with one mighty effort straight from the shoulder he connected with the door which, under this attack, immediately splintered and gave way in much less time than by using a key. The door was not the only thing that suffered as poor Kirby also fractured his wrist. However, this seemed of no concern to him so long as we could proceed with the rehearsal.

Colonel Kirby took much interest in woodwork and engineering and after leaving Minety in 1935 he carried on his hobbies at Portcullis House, Acton Turville, where no doubt to satisfy a whim he built a huge yacht on the lawn. Whether he ever took the yacht to the water or brought the water to the yacht is one thing I never knew.

During the 1940's Minety House was occupied for a very short while consecutively by Mr. Douglas West and Miss Lawson until in 1947 Major and Mrs. Crocker bought the estate, which had by this time dwindled to less than a hundred acres. During the time of his residence much of the Minety land and many of the farms were restored so that Minety House is now the largest estate in the parish consisting of more than 700 acres.

Minety House had its own private piped water supply before the mains were brought to the village. It was a well-devised system arranged by digging a reservoir by the "Fox Cover" and the water piped more than a quarter-of-a-mile across the road to the house, the water flowing by gravity as the reservoir was on much higher ground. This was mostly surface water and so as to augment the supply a large area of ground was covered with corrugated iron to catch rain water which was directed to the reservoir. This was in the field where Major Gouldsmith had spent much time and money laying out a cricket pitch which was drained by cinders laid under the turf. It was the duty of the local lads to keep the pitch rolled and many an hour have I spent there helping to pull and push a heavy two-horse iron flat roll back and forth before an evening's practice. A sound I shall always remember is the resounding echo of the cricket ball when it landed on the corrugated iron of the reservoir or the galvanised roof of the pavilion. All this is now but a memory.

Major and Mrs. Crocker have always shown great interest in the affairs of the village and have wrought many changes for its benefit. They have been large employers of labour, built houses and given generously of their time and money on the St. Leonard's Church. They were also largely instrumental by generous contributions in making it possible to rebuild the Village Hall to modern standards. This alone should stand for generations and be an outward and visible sign of their generosity to the community in general.

Hovington House

HOVINGTON HOUSE, which stands adjacent to St. Leonard's Church and School, stands on the site of what was without doubt one of the oldest houses in the parish.

Legend has it that many years ago it was inhabited by priests and that an underground passage communicated from there to the church.

Hovington House, Minety.

On the old Ordnance Survey Map of 1838 it seems that most, if not all, of the property was glebe land. Known in the last century as Church Farm it was occupied by Daniel Reynolds—who was my wife's great-grandfather. According to Mercer & Crocker's Directory, he was there in 1874 until Mark Lewis, who was my uncle, came there from Turk's Farm, Charlton, which he had rented from the Earl of Suffolk at a yearly rental of £66-7-0d. Mark Lewis was there until 1891, when he took over the tenancy of Swillbrook Farm, previously occupied by Mrs. Anna Coole on a tenancy from Mrs. Brewin who owned several farms in this district. Then came Lewington Howse, whose mother before her marriage was Ellen Manners.

As many of the old directories give only the names of occupiers and not their place of residence, it is very difficult to make a complete record of some places.

The original house possibly dated back to mediaeval times as there is still evidence of a moat on the eastern side.

Until the first decade of the 20th century there was a small cottage just inside the entrance gates on the left. There lived Ann Jerome, the village midwife and "blood-letter" as she was known, this being a remedy for most ailments in those days.

However, one thing is certain and that is that Lewington Howse was tenant there until towards the end of the 19th century, when the house was purchased by Charles Frederick Moore, of the old established firm of Moore, Allen and Innocent. C. F. Moore had the house entirely rebuilt, using the old stone as far as possible from the original house which had resembled a chapel in some parts. This feature has been rebuilt into the house as it stands today. This supports the theory that at some time, very many years ago, it was part of or connected with the church.

Many of the men engaged walked from Ashton Keynes and I remember my old friend Benjamin Greenslade recall how he had seen them walking past his home—Telling's Farm—one behind the other, "duck fashion" as he amusingly described it.

"Little Alice" Telling, not much over four feet tall, a faithful Church worker and Sunday School teacher, only recently passed to Higher Service, used to tell of her late husband Herbie Telling having the job of mixing mortar for the builders.

Perhaps due to the fact that Mr. Moore was spending so much money on improving the property, it became known at the time as "Moore's Folly." The result however of all this expenditure was a beautiful residence equal to any in the district. C. F. Moore was not the man to make a hasty decision and it very shortly became known as "St. Leonard's Hall." However, it was Frederick Moore himself who first referred to it as "Moore's Folly," but it was a gamble that paid off.

It is said that there were two fonts in the old farmhouse, one of which he gave to the church, the other being built into the new house which was erected between 1895 and 1897.

Viscount Trafalgar resided there for a short time at the turn of the century before taking over Braydon Hall.

Captain Mayall lived there until 1911. For a time it was occupied by Bertie Smith who was rather eccentric and always seemed to be riding around on a bicycle with a hammock seat. In 1925 Mrs. Perry took up residence and after her, I believe, Tom Bishell who again named it Church Farm and milked a herd of cows, retailing some of the milk around the village. He was an army officer standing six feet tall or more and he drove one of the first "Austin 7's". As can be imagined, it was a case of "much in little" as when driving his knees came up each side of the steering wheel. It was a mystery how he ever managed to extricate himself. I will add however, in fairness to him, that he also owned one of the best cars on the road at that time, a "Hillman Straight 8" and he would demonstrate how he could accelerate from a standing start in top gear.

After him, in quick succession, came a Mr. and Mrs. Atkinson and a Mr. Baker, until in 1935 the property was bought by Captain Geof. Hovington Raimes. Captain Raimes was a very active supporter of the Church, the Conservative Party and the British Legion, being Chairman of the Minety Branch of the British Legion from 1947 to 1969. It was he who was largely instrumental in organising the purchase and erection of a large ex-W.D. nissen hut which was dismantled at Cricklade and re-erected near Minety Station to serve as British Legion Headquarters, which it did for many years. The whole of the operation was performed voluntarily by members of the branch. The hut contained a club room with a full-sized billiards table (kindly given by the late Bishop Ramsey), a skittle alley and rifle range, which was backed up with several yards of sand and ½in. iron plates which had been used during the war as protection on the railway carriage used by General Eisenhower when he was successfully conducting military operations on the continent up to the conclusion of hostilities.

In 1951 when His Majesty King George VI reviewed a march-past of the British Legion in Hyde Park, our standard bearer found at the last minute that he would be unable to take part. Captain Raimes rang me up to ask if I would fill the gap. We called and collected the Standard and letter of instructions which we could not read until we were on the train when we discovered to our dismay that white gauntlet gloves were to be worn. We had none, neither had we any opportunity of obtaining any. Fortunately Captain Raimes had two tickets for the stand close to the royal dais where we had to be content to sit and watch all the other contingents march past with their standards whilst ours was lying rolled up in its case in the "left luggage" office at Paddington Station.

This was a day to be remembered in more ways than one. Captain Raimes son, William, came with us as far as Paddington as the A.A.A. Championships were in full swing at the White City and his programme was to spend the day there and to meet us at Paddington in the evening.

After the Hyde Park ceremony, Captain Raimes and I had time to look around, and decided to spend an hour at the Royal Academy which was then open. There were many masterpieces there by the very foremost artists of the day.

At this time my wife's uncle, Mr. Harold Kinch, had recently retired from farming and was living in Cirencester (Chesterton). Opposite to him lived that great portrait painter, the late F. Cadogan Cowper, R.A., who had asked my uncle if he would sit for a portrait. Imagine my surprise when in Gallery No. 7 there looking down on us from picture No. 379 entitled "The Featherbed Farmer" was Harold Kinch, among the famous, with a look in his eyes as if to say "What are you doing here?" and I am sure that if he could have seen my eyes they would have been echoing those very words.

Besides being a successful farmer, Harold Kinch was also a good sportsman and quite capable of looking on the humourous side of being described as a "Featherbed Farmer." If any man could work seven days a week on a farm, as he had done for sixty years, and come through with a smile on his face he deserved a feather bed!

We must not forget that when this country was at war it was men like him who were producing the food that saved us from starvation.

Did not Napoleon Bonaparte utter those very true words that "an army marches on its stomach"? This applies not only to the soldiers but equally to everyone who hopes to survive.

*　　*　　*　　*

Braydon Hall

BRAYDON HALL, one of the stately homes of Minety, is shown in the Survey of 1773 by Andrews and Dury as "Pound House." Facing Minety Common as it does, it could be that it was here that any animals straying from the Common

"The Featherbed Farmer."
A pencil sketch from the portrait in oils by F. Cadogan Cowper, R.A. Exhibited
at the Royal Academy in 1951. This is a portrait of Mr. Harold Kinch of Fyfield,
Glos., who farmed at Thornhill Farm, Lechlade.

could be impounded by the Lord of the Manor and held until a fine had been paid by the unfortunate owner to obtain their release.

There is a plaque on one of the walls in the house which bears the following inscription:—

"George Pitt Efqre Lord of this Mannor
erected Braydon House
in the year of our Lord 1751
Mr. Willm Leanes being then Steward
Jafper Yorke Surveyor
Mr. Henry & Joseph Maskelyne
Tenants of the Estates
Anthony Norton Carpenter"

Braydon Hall.

According to old title deeds of properties in Minety a Joseph Pitt was Lord of the Manor of Minety in 1841 and Richard Mullings deputy Steward. However in a document dated December 13rd, 1871 Arthur Randolph Mullings was Lord of the Manor. The Manor was still held by the Mullings family at least until Richard Mullings died in 1956 and probably still is.

I have a photostat copy of the first accurate Tithe Map of this district which I obtained from the Archivist, Wilts County Offices, Trowbridge, dated 1839 which shows the Keenes as being the chief land owners. Both Braydon Hall Estate and Minety House Estate were held by them, the former owned by one Joseph Keene and the latter by the representatives of William Keene. The Keene family owned property in Minety from at least the eighteenth century and there are tombs in Minety Churchyard recording deaths from 1796 if not earlier and to a Mary, wife of Thomas Keene, who died at Braydon House, March 3rd 1879, aged eighty-seven years.

12

After the Keenes came Mrs. Fitzgerald, who was there in 1884, followed by the Scotts. The Minety ratebook for 1900 gives Henry Workman as being the owner and Mrs. Amelia Scott the tenant of Braydon Hall estate of 142 acres; Distillery Farm of 76 acres, one rood, 5 poles; Braydon Hall Woods and Plantations 62 acres; comprising together about 270 acres.

The Scott family however were in residence until the end of the reign of Queen Victoria, as it was Mrs. Scott who came to the Silver Street School on the accession of King Edward VII and presented each child with a Coronation Medal. I am proud to say that I still have mine in my possession. I can vaguely remember her producing them one at a time from a cardboard box. I was taken by my mother to the coronation festivities which were held in Braydon Park. I was a very small child at the time and all the womenfolk wore long, black shiny skirts. I, being little more than knee high, had as much as I could do holding on to my mother's skirt in the crowd. As was to be expected we were forced apart, as, having occasion to make some remark to my mother and tugging at the skirt to draw her attention I noticed to my dismay that the face that looked down at me was that of a complete stranger. Where my mother was I had not the faintest idea. My usual practice in such circumstances was to yell, which I did, and the noise soon brought my lost parent on the scene and peace was once again restored.

In 1903 Viscount and Lady Trafalgar were living at Braydon Hall. They were followed by Colonel Pym who, while he was there was largely responsible for raising a troop of volunteers for the Wilts Yeomanry which he trained in the Park. He, however left before the 1914-18 War and was followed at the Hall by Captain James who had one daughter, a son and three step-daughters.

In the early part of the war the Royal Flying Corps were in training at Upavon, Netheravon and Yatesbury and as many of the officers were known at Braydon Hall and also at the Vicarage (the vicar's son, Sir Edgar Rainey Ludlow Hewitt had joined the Royal Flying Corps) great excitement was caused at weekends when one or two of these ancient flying machines or "string bags" as they were called would land at Braydon Hall, sometimes in the Park on Husk Hill and in the small fields adjoining. Although they always managed to take off it was said at the time that one aircraft lost a wheel clearing the woods to the south of the Park. Whether it made a happy landing we never knew.

There was always a crowd of local people standing around to watch the take-off.

Soon after the end of World War I Captain and Mrs. James both having died, and some of the daughters married, the Hall again became vacant. A Mr. and Mrs. Harrison lived there for a few years until it was bought by Mr. Fred Ziegler in 1925. In 1936 the Hall again changed hands, this time to Major Barrington Chance. At the time of writing Major and Mrs. Chance are still in residence.

Braydon Hall was one of the first houses to have a piped water supply. A reservoir was dug in the Park about three hundred yards from the house which was supplied by surface water coming down from the Common. From the time I was a boy until the 1920's an oil engine was housed there to pump the water to the house. However, when Mr. Fred Ziegler bought the property he drilled for water and water was found which was pumped to the tank mounted on a high structure on Husk Hill, from whence it flowed by gravity to the house and buildings.

This water was found to be very hard and before it could be used it was necessary to pass it through a "water softener" containing caustic soda. Many a ton of this did I transport from Minety Station during his residence. It was packed in sealed circular containers, each holding half a hundredweight.

This independent water supply was not however required after about 1937 when the local authorities brought mains water to the district.

At this period the Electricity Board had not come to Minety and those householders who had electric lighting had to run their own generating plant. Braydon

13

Hall had what I should consider the largest and most efficient lighting plant in the district. With Mr. Ziegler money seemed to be in plentiful supply. This lighting plant was of 100 volts, powered by a Ruston & Hornsby 6 h.p. horizontal single cylinder oil engine which was started up by heating the hotplate with a blow-lamp. The flywheel was about five feet in diameter. The engine being mounted on a concrete bed about one foot in height meant that the flywheel was let into the ground for clearance. In the wall of the engine room was a vertical slot so that the belt could be used to drive a circular saw in the woodshed. and so make the most possible use of the engine. This was before the Southern Electricity Board came into being and the first mains electricity came to the village in 1947 when this area was covered by the Wessex Electricity Company.

For two or three decades dating from about the turn of the century, acetylene gas was used for lighting many of the big houses, also cars and motor cycles were lit by gas. Carbide was used for this and when water was allowed to drop on to it a very inflammable gas was given off. The rate of flow of the water was controlled by a needle valve through the water chamber operated by hand.

Early in the century Cirencester was supplied with electric light and power by a firm named Edwards and Armstrong, who had premises off Gloucester Street. This was direct current and not alternating as it is today. Their dynamos were driven by a Producer Gas engine, an Allen semi-diesel and a huge vertical cylinder "Ricardo" Submarine engine of Italian make. "Ricardo's" also turned out a motor cycle engine which was at one time fitted to some "Triumph" models.

In about 1930 Edwards and Armstrong became the Wessex Electricity Company and later when electricity was nationalised they became known as the Electricity Board.

The present supply, which is of 230-40 volts, is suitable for all purposes, both power and lighting and is, of course, much more economical than using an independent generating unit.

Before taking over Braydon Hall, Lord and Lady Trafalgar lived for a short time at Church Farm, Minety, which stood opposite St. Leonard's Church, where Hovington House now stands. The old farmhouse stood lower down, behind St. Leonard's School.

Lord Trafalgar was quite a character. At the time he lived at Church Farm, my Uncle Herbert Manners was farming at Vicarage Farm which he rented from William Oliver, Esq., of The Mansells.

One day His Lordship strolled across to have a few words with my Uncle, which he was often wont to do. Noticing that my uncle was smoking his pipe he jocularly remarked, "I see you have your pipe on the go Manners, you can't smoke too much, but you can drink too much." This theory he demonstrated in no uncertain manner and my cousin Percy often had to see him safely home when he left for Braydon Hall. In appreciation of this Lady Trafalgar once gave Percy a locker which she said had belonged to Lord Nelson of Trafalgar.

Old Fred Hughes once told me the tale that one night he had been up to the "Old Inn" just to have a drop himself before it was all gone. He came across the Village Green and down the cinder track from Home Farm, striking the lower Minety road just above Fishponds Woods. As he approached the road he heard someone calling as though in distress. In the roadside ditch was Lord Trafalgar who, it appeared, was returning from Minety House where, it would seem, he had "dined not wisely but too well." Said Fred, "The only thing I could do was to get him on his hind legs and help him home." This act of kindness on old Fred's part did not go unrewarded, for to his great surprise, when they arrived at Braydon Hall, to use Fred's words, "He put his hand in his pocket and gid ma a gold half-sovereign." No wonder old Fred remembered that night. However, living up to his reputation, the story is that in the end he fell down the cellar steps at Braydon Hall with fatal results. This is the story as I have heard it but I cannot vouch for the truth of it.

14

A book could be written on Braydon Hall alone. Mr. Fred Ziegler, who bought it just after World War I, spent many thousands of pounds on enlarging the house, installing electric light, building stables and garages, a huge rockery to the west and two large summer houses flanking the front entrance. These were built with the Cotswold Stone from a cottage which stood at Poole Keynes for several hundred years. At that time, in the late 1920's, I was in business with Phil Miles, trading as "Miles and Manners, Garage Proprietors" with cars for hire and hauling undertaken. I moved the whole of that cottage to Minety, throwing every stone up by hand and unloading it at Braydon Hall where the builders were using it up almost as fast as I could get it to them. I found out long afterwards that the men demolishing the cottage were supposed to be helping in the loading of the stone. They must have known that I was ignorant of the fact as they never once gave me a hand.

The stone pillars at the entrance to the Hall originally stood at Distillery Farm and an exchange was negotiated whereby the wooden gate and ornamental railings each side of it be taken to Distillery Farm and the stone pillars from there to Braydon Hall. I was also responsible for the hauling involved with this.

The Rockery was built with rock from Minchinhampton Common and that neighbourhood and I soon found that a heavier vehicle would be required so that had to be completed by another contractor.

The Nott Stone

The Braydon Hall Estate was at one time almost in the centre of Braydon Forest. An interesting event which happened in the eighteenth century is recorded on a stone which still stands in Ravensroost Woods. It appears that at that time there was a firm of Court Tailors by the name of Knott. Some member of the Royal Family (as many still do) had fallen into arrears with his account and was forced to find some solution to the problem of satisfying the tailor. To this end, so the story goes, he gave to the Nott family a portion of the forest to settle the account. A stone was erected to mark the dividing line with the following inscription engraved on it:—

THIS WOOD DIVIDED IN 1770 BY
CAPT. JOHN H. NOTT OF THE ROYAL NAVY

The stone stands about fifty yards inside the gate on the east side of the wood near the Minety to Brinkworth road.

The accompanying plan gives directions as to its whereabouts. The Farm, now known as Ravenshurst which lies about half a mile to the south, was then known as Knott's Farm and there is a field nearby which is still called "The Tailor's."

QUOTING from Dr. T. R. Thomson's *History of Bradon Forest*," pages 28—30.

"Roger Nott, Citizen and Merchant Tailor was granted 360 acres of Duchy land (i.e. 2 portions) and 430 acres of Exchequer land.

The latter was the Great or Old Lodge land and part of Tollenthresh Hill. The lodge was later known as Nott's House. The moat, close to Ravenshurst Farm, may yet be seen.

Nott was trustee for his son's wife's father Edward Sewster, Gent, of Huntingdon who became demented in 1638. How much money, if any, the king owed for clothes is unknown.

Roger Nott seems to have been an unpleasant and grasping tradesman of unascertained origin. He was the founder of a family who yet survive.

The third lease was granted to James Duart. The lodge concerned was Sliford's Lodge afterwards called Slifield Lodge and now known as Leighfield Lodge. The lease was for 586 acres of Duchy land (i.e. two portions and the

15

Portion of Braydon Forest given to the Notts (Court Tailors) to settle accounts.

Duchy Rag) and 695 acres of Exchequer land. The latter was made up of the original 430 Slyford quarter with some of the remainder of the unleased Ravenshurst White Spire quarter."

The subsequent history of the holding is as follows. (Still quoting from Dr. Thomson's book.)

"Frances Jacobsen, widow of Philip Jacobson obtained a confirmation of lease from Lady Day (March 25th) 1668 but the acreage was less than that of the original. In 1697 on the expiration of the original lease, King William III granted a lease in reverse of expectation on the life of Queen Catherine to Paul Jodrel Esquire of the Inner Temple. In 1743-4 Robert Neale, a relative of the Notts, petitioned for a reversionary lease. In 1805 James Cochran leased it. In 1815 the Earl of Clarendon became owner by exchange with the Crown. Most of this property was acquired by Joseph NEALE, Solicitor (1754-1828) and was inherited by his son, John NEELD, who was created a baronet in 1859 and sat as one of the members of Parliament for Cricklade. Red Lodge was purchased by John Edward Ward, Solicitor in 1901 and is now the residence of Harold Rogers Ward, J.P., Barrister at Law of the Inner Temple. It is not known when the present Red Lodge was built. The name has not been found before 1711, the date of Edward Nott's will. The 180 acre strip of land on which it stands consists of an upper or north part known as Battle End, a middle part known as Longupshill and a southern part, Bernewood. In the *Valuation of Crown Lands* 1649-59 the name of H. Pretty stands against Longupshill Lodge. This is undoubtedly the site of Red Lodge.

Webb's Lodge or Hatton's Lodge occupied the site of White Lodge, now Red Lodge Farm. The present White Lodge is near the old White Lodge Farm.

Reverting to the Great Lodge Holding, we find that in 1651 Edward Nott, described as "guardian of Braydon with others" received a further lease of a 'Portion' of 180 acres of Duchy land and 80 acres of Exchequer land from Queen Catherine.

In 1696 this was leased to him for thirty years, probably at the time when the original lease was renewed. This is, however, a matter of some uncertainty. In spite of Strangers' petitions the Notts held on.

In 1786 Catherine, widow of Commander John Neale Pleydell Nott, R.N. held a Bradon lease. Slyfield Lodge is apparently that property known in the *Valuation of Crown Lands* as Creekland. The name of the occupier was G. Vaux, etc. It is almost certain that Vaux and Duart were partners as in 1676 a Mr. Duart held the property or some moiety thereof. The holding passed into the hands of the Huppisley Cox family and was bought in 1817 by Michael Poole and Jos Poole Junr. at the same time that the latter bought the original 430 acres of Exchequer land leased in 1637 to Roger Nott."

Although this book is not intended to be a history I have to mention at some point or other, incidents connected with the Great War of 1914-18. This one in particular I think is worth recording as it is in connection with Red Lodge.

Before the final offensive on the Western Front in August 1918 my battery of Royal Field Artillery had been withdrawn from the line for two or three weeks' refresher training for "open warfare" as opposed to "trench warfare." For this we went into Belgium, near Provens. The offensive was due to commence on August 8th, which incidentally was my 21st birthday.

On the Sunday morning previous to our departure a Service was held in a large barn there. Being fully aware of the uncertainty of what might be ahead of us I decided I would remain for the Communion Service when the Chaplain invited those wishing to receive the Holy Sacrement to remain in their seats. I soon found myself sitting alone in the barn but the Padre started the Service as though the place had been full. When it was over he came to me to have a few words which I thought was very kind of him. I do not remember what he asked me but no sooner had I answered him than he said, "You come from the South." I said, "Yes Sir. From Minety in Wiltshire." Imagine my astonishment when he said "Oh! I know Minety very well. I've walked down the line from Red Lodge to Minety Station many a time." As he was a commissioned officer I just could not bring myself to ask his name although I never forgot the incident.

Little did I know then that there was a shell waiting with "my name on it" and that shortly after this incident I was to collect a piece of it in my right arm during the attack on St. Quentin on September 27th, 1918.

This piece of shrapnel I still keep as a memento, wrapped in a piece of bandage as it was given to me by the orderly at Rouen No. 26 General Hospital.

Many years later, during the 1939-45 War, I happened to meet Captain Harold

Ward at a farm sale and told him the story. "Oh!" he said, "Grice Hutchinson. My wife's brother and he's grumbling now because they won't have him in this war." That was the type of man he was. Since then I have met him more-than once and have read his book on his experiences in France. This I found particularly interesting because he was Chaplain to 168 Brigade in which I served as a Signaller.

The Mansells

"MYNTYE" OR "MINTY" now spelt "MINETY" was so named because much wild mint grew here. This is no news to many who have studied books on Wiltshire, but to others this may be of importance. Living as I did at the Moor for so many years I remember it could be found growing by the brook which runs from Minety to Ashton Keynes. More than likely there are many other places where it still grows.

Many of the farms and fields take their names from previous owners or occupiers. For instance there is Rigsby Lane between Minety and Oaksey. In the Oaksey Rate Book of 1842 William Rigsby is named as owning a cottage and garden and fifteen perches of land—number 284 in the book. There could be a connection here. The Ordnance Survey Map of 1925 gives "Rudge," "Rough" or "Ridge" Lane as Rigsby's Lane. These are two entirely different lanes and the Minety Rate Book of 1900 describes all the properties (and there were at least half a dozen) as adjoining "Rough Lane." This was without doubt an old Roman Road as it runs along the ridge, which is characteristic.

"The Mansells" is undoubtedly the oldest building apart from the Church in Minety and is thought to have been occupied at one time by William Penn.

The Mansells, Minety.

The origin of its name is still wrapt in mystery. The Standard Dictionary describes a Manse as a house belonging to a Church for a Clergyman. According to the St. Leonard's Church Register a certain John Mansell was living in Minety in 1691, the Baptism of a son John is entered and also the burial of a John Mansell, Ironmonger, in 1702. It is quite possible that it could have been the home of the Mansell family.

Also in the Church Register there is an entry of the Baptism of John, son of John and Mary Pitman in 1666. Whether they lived at the Mansells I cannot say nor to which of these families the initials over one of the doors may apply. Someone else may solve that one.

18

Farmhouses

IT is quite likely that many of the farmhouses are named after their one-time occupants such as Telling's Farm which belonged to Henry Telling in 1838. Hawkin's Lane adjoined land owned by a J. Hawkins; Coole's Farm after the Cooles family and Buckswell farm was undoubtedly named after the well which was sunk many years ago. The owner at that time hoped to make a fortune by selling the water which was thought to contain valuable medicinal properties. This was presumably a failure as not much has been heard of it since. Some "very strong water" is however mentioned in John Aubrey's book on Wiltshire which he found in a "place called the Bogges beside the Malmesbury to Ashton Keynes road on Minety Common."

The "Three Bridges" between Ashton Keynes and Minety on the boundary of Braydon Forest, showing the old ford. Before bridge and ford were demolished in 1969. Ref. S.U.044934

I have probably made mistakes in my own book, but trying to locate this particular spot is rather a problem. It is known that Aubrey was not always correct. I do know however that on the Elms Farm towards Woburn there is a field known as "The Bog Ground" of about six acres and very wet. There is also a pool there. Going back to the Survey of 1773 there was a road from Bullock's Horn to Woburn and thence to Minety. These roads no longer exist although traces are visible. We do not know which road he took from Malmesbury but if he took the old Coach Road he would have come by Somerford Common and perhaps Minety Common. There is said to be salt water in a pool on Somerford Common. Aubrey says that he boiled a sample and there were crystals left in the bottom of the pan. As there were then many and various ways of getting from Malmesbury to Ashton Keynes one cannot be sure whether he took his sample from here and proceeded to Minety Common which adjoins, whether he took it from the "Bog Ground" at Woburn in Hankerton Common or from "Buck's Well." He could even have found himself on Minety Moor which runs from the railway east to Ashton Keynes. Very strange it is that the highest part of the Moor is known as Lower Moor. There is the Lower Moor Farm, then lower down the Moor Farm. Lower still is Field Farm, which, in the 1900 Rate book is called "Upper Moor Farm." Next comes "The Moor Ground" of about five acres, and a quarter-of-a-mile further on towards Ashton is "Moor Leaze Farm." I should say that Minety Moor dissolved into Ashton Keynes Moor because the first large field is called "South Moor" although this is not in Minety parish.

Going back to Minety Common there is "New House Farm"—possibly built after the Common was enclosed. Further south there is "Southend Farm" probably meaning the southern end of the Common.

Half a mile further on and lying back from the road is what was once known as "Nott's Farm." This was part of the land included in the settlement when the Ravensroost Woods were divided (as described elsewhere) but is now known as "Ravenshurst Farm."

There is a Silver Street at Minety. Historians say that wherever there is a street of this name the locality has been inhabited from very earliest times.

Sawyer's Hill I just venture a guess at but it is a fact that for very many years this part of Minety has been the home of carpenters and sawyers. I myself can remember seeing men working in the old sawpit by the Askew Bridge when Maurice Henry Miles lived there at the turn of the century. One man would stand in the pit below ground and the other on the tree trunk which was laid length-wise, often sawing out coffin boards. They sawed to a chalk line which was made by rubbing white chalk on a string. Stretching it from end to end and pulling it like a bowstring, when it struck the timber it left a white line as straight as an arrow.

There also lived at the bottom of Sawyer's Hill, opposite Frogmore, a man named John Randall. He too was a carpenter and sawyer. He was born in a cottage between Cooles Farm and the railway. He was the son of John Chapple Randall who married a Mary Read at Minety Church on October 8th, 1832. John Randall, the son, was sometimes called John Chapple. No wonder then, what with the Primitive Methodist Chapel at the top of the hill and John Chapple living at the bottom, Sawyers Hill was often spoken of as Chapel Hill.

The old cottage at Cooles where John Randall was born was called "The Owl's Nest." It was well off the beaten track although before the railway was built it was accessible from Ruddock's Lane which led to Oaksey. When old John Chapple Randall died at the "Owl's Nest" from a heart attack it was said that he had been chopping wood on a Sunday. My father used to say to me, "You must never work on the Sabbath. Old John Randall dropped dead through chopping wood on a Sunday."

One might wonder at a farm being named "Distillery Farm." This was not without good reason as it was proposed at one time to use the place as a distillery. This project must have fallen through like many other ambitious schemes.

At Upper Minety there is "Mill Farm." The story goes that it was intended by the owner some hundred or so years ago to erect a mill and carry on business as a miller. However as funds began to run short the mill was never completed, neither was the dwelling house for many years after.

The "Elms Farm" was, before the 1914-18 war almost hidden by enormous elm trees. During the war and owing to a shortage of timber caused by the blockade all available trees were felled. Flistridge Woods suffered greatly. Most of the elms were cut on Elms Farm. The timber was transported to Minety Station by Austin Clarke who then farmed Osborne's Farm. It was all drawn by horse teams and timber carriages with iron tyres. By the end of the war the road from Flistridge to Minety Station was cut into ruts two to three feet deep so that it was not safe to ride a bicycle. This included Silver Street and it was impossible for a farmer to drive a horse and crank axle milk cart, the ruts being so deep that the axle dragged on the ridge between them.

After the war a sawmill was set up on the Elms Farm and yet more trees were felled and sawn into boards, posts, stakes and rails. I bought several loads for the Moor Farm and I believe I could still identify some of it.

"Gibb's Farm" probably belonged to a man of that name. Yet another farm, "Elizabeth's Farm" was no doubt so named for the same reason. It was practically cut in half by the railway line as it extended over an area running from the Moor to Silver Street. "London Lane" which runs from the Malmesbury Road to "Duchy Rag," Chelworth and Purton was also severed and the bridle track diverted to lead in from the opposite or east side of the railway.

You do occasionally hear of a house being moved from one place to another, but very seldom is a farm house moved ftom one parish to another. Just before the First World War, a house which stood in the parish of Hankerton was purchased by the late Mr. Albert Prior of Shades Farm, Minety, and re-erected on land on the opposite side of the road to his farm where there were other farm buildings. This was then named Grange Farm. The house was constructed of timber and corrugated iron.

* * * *

DURING 1947 a list was made under Section 30 of the "Town and Country Planning Act" of any buildings of Special Architectural or Historical Interest which by (or under) this Act are scheduled to be preserved so as to retain some of the local character of the countryside.

There are five buildings to my knowledge in Minety on this list, viz:—
"Flistridge Farm House," "The Mansells," "The Old Inn," "Minety House" and "Moor Farm House,"

therefore it is very appropriate to mention here that Flistridge Farm House was my birthplace, where I lived until 1899 when my father left there and took the tenancy of the Moor Farm, the owner at that time being Samuel Clappen of Cirencester.

In 1919 the Moor Farm was sold by public auction at the King's Head, Cirencester, when my father became the owner. The whole of my farming career was spent there, the mortgage being eventually paid off in 1947, when through

The Moor Farm, Minety.

ill-health, I was forced to cease farming activities I left my elder son, John, in possession. He was able to buy the property in 1965, so becoming the third generation of Manners' to own the farm. Also another Henry Manners, a relative of my father, had occupied the farm in the 1860's as a tenant farmer.

Copy of Notice

IMPORTANT. This communication affects your Property.

TOWN AND COUNTRY PLANNING ACT, 1947

SECTION 30

BUILDINGS OF SPECIAL ARCHITECTURAL OR HISTORIC INTEREST

To: L. J. Manners, Esq.,
          Moor Farmhouse,
             Minety, Malmesbury, Wilts.

NOTICE IS HEREBY GIVEN that the building known as Moor Farmhouse, Minety, situate in the Rural District of Malmesbury, has been included in the list of buildings of special Architectural or Historical Interest in that area compiled by the Minister of Housing and Local Government on the 28th October, 1959.

E. H. T. WILTSHIRE

Authorised by the Minister to sign in that behalf.
Dated this 13th day of November 1959.

From the Ministry of Housing and Local Government,
       31/34, Chester Terrace,
           Regent's Park, N.W.1.
H.B.15.   Reference 2228/11/A.

This part of Wiltshire has undoubtedly been inhabited from the very earliest times. While digging an air raid shelter during World War II a bronze hammer head was found which has been sent to Malmesbury for identification. Several 17th century coins have also come to light, fortunately in a good state of preservation, and a halfpenny bronze token bearing the name of John Starr of Kemble, dated 1667 were dug up in the garden.

Plank Stone and Rail.
Many of these stiles still exist though in many cases the plank stones have now been replaced by rails and the plankstones used for covering drockways.

Several windows of the farmhouse had been walled in to avoid payment of the "Window" tax which was still in force from 1696 to 1851. One of these is still to be seen. There are two bread ovens in the walls, a pair of millstones was found under the pantry floor and built into the front of the house, about shoulder high, there is an old "Priest's Dial" or "Scratch Dial" cut into what appears to be a buttress stone thought to have been salvaged from Cirencester Abbey after its destruction. It is well known that the sites of demolished monastries and churches were at that time used as quarries by the local builders, apparently without let or hindrance, so that bits and pieces are found in many of these old buildings.

There was at one time a very fine pair of Sarcen Stone pillars, five or six feet in height, and weighing many hundredweights. One of these is still in existence. There was also a heavy stone shaped for a cheese press weighing two or three hundredweight. This has become very worn and damaged, having been used by many generations as a stand for the washtub. It still has the rusty remains of the suspending irons held in by pouring in molten lead.

From the large amount of old pottery that is continually coming to light it is quite possible that there could have been a kiln there very many years ago.

The pattern on some of the more decorative pieces which I have in my museum appears to have been made with a pointed stick and the thumb with many impressions of the tip of the finger or thumbnail. Whilst cutting a hedge by "Rudge" or "Ridge" Lane, part of an ancient wooden beamed plough was found in the bank. It appears to be the portion used for adjusting the width of the furrow but has become very rusty and corroded.

Cooles Farmhouse.

This picture of Cooles Farmhouse shews, on the right, the well that I fell down when I was two years old, as mentioned elsewhere. Cooles is one of the few remaining houses with a dormer window to the cheese room, and is shewn on the first accurate survey map made by Andrews and Dury in 1773.

My Grandfather started his farming career at Cooles in 1840. I still have a copy of the Tenancy Agreement dated September 3rd of that year, the tenancy commencing on September 29th. My Grandparents were then minors, my Grandfather being only eighteen years of age. They were referred to at that time as "the children." The agreement therefore had to be signed by their parents and read "as between David Whatley of Cirencester, Gentleman, of the one part and John Manners of Calstone near Calne, in the County of Wilts, Farmer, and Joseph Maundrell of Calne aforesaid Butcher and on behalf of Edward Manners son of the above named John Manners at present under age, of the other part."

The Railway, opened in 1843, passed through the farm and cut off any access to land which he occupied on the other side of the line. This meant he would be obliged to take his cattle on the road and over the level crossing at Brandiers in order to reach it. This the landlord would not allow claiming that "by taking the cattle on the road the manurial value of their droppings would be lost to the land."

Cooles Farmhouse is now the property of my son, Rodney Henry Eddolls Manners, he being the fourth generation of the Manners family to live there.

Gospel Oak

ABOUT two miles south of Minety stands a red brick farmhouse known as Gospel Oak. My first recollection of it is during the first decade of this century when a cousin of mine named Roger Howse was the tenant. His mother was my father's eldest sister, Ellen Manners. Apparently the farm was sold to a Mr. Jull and rumour had it that he was a German. It was a fact that a man named Von Haast had bought property in the vicinity and so of course when war broke out in 1914, all sorts of tales began flying around especially as the improvements carried out at Gospel Oak included the building of a high tower, and the house is situated on high ground with a fine view south over the Wiltshire and Berkshire Downs and north over the Cotswolds and beyond. Among the rumours was one that "wireless" was being used to send messages to Germany—and these rumours persisted.

"Pinch Belly" type of stile of which many may still be found. Where there were carriageways with ten foot gates, these stiles were often added to save pedestrians from having to open the gates and thus obviate the risk of gates being left open allowing animals to stray. In some cases a step was fixed to the gate where there was no stile.

It appeared that Jull had come to this country from Australia. He had grand ideas of making money and had converted the farmhouse into a hostel with extensive sleeping and living accommodation with a view to running it as a training college for farm students under the grand name of "The Gospel Oak Colonial Training College" and it was not long before it was filled with students of many nationalities. And now we come to the climax of the story.

It was in 1918. I was in France but my two younger brothers were at home at the Moor Farm. The elder of them, Edward, had been to an entertainment or dance one evening, arriving home soon after midnight and feeling rather tired. He happened to look out of the window and saw what appeared to him to be a light presumably from a vehicle which had stopped on the road opposite the house. Not wanting to be kept out of bed any longer he quietly crept upstairs to the room which he shared with the younger brother, Harry, who was fast asleep. On looking out of the bedroom window he could see that the light was further away than he had thought and in order to get a better view he opened the window, climbed partly out on to the window sill and having satisfied himself that it was probably a house or hayrick on fire in the distance, he started to climb back into the bedroom.

Young Harry, awakened by the noise, opened his eyes to see what he immediately thought was an intruder breaking into the house. His first thought was to shout at the top of his voice, "Dad! Bring the gun!" scared almost out of his wits. It was some time before the situation could be explained and peace again restored.

Next day we heard that the fire was actually Gospel Oak burning. The cause of the fire or any details of it were never generally known. If there ever was any signalling apparatus there, the evidence was completely destroyed by the fire. The story as I heard it was that Mr. Jull himself was away at the time. The fire broke out late at night and Mrs. Jull ran across to "Red Lodge" which is opposite in her night clothes. Captain Ward, who lived at "Red Lodge" with his wife, happened to be home on leave from his regiment and having a car, immediately rushed off to Cricklade for the fire engine. There were then no telephones available and the fire engine was horse-drawn.

"The Swing or Clap Gate." This means of access was often used instead of a gate. While it prevents animals from straying it allows pedestrians to pass through by swinging the gate. It was much favoured by the Railway Companies at one time but with steel tubing in place of the wooden rails.

On arrival at Cricklade, Captain Ward found the captain of the fire brigade and asked for immediate help. "Well," said he, "We shan't be able to come tonight. The horses are turned out in North Meadow and we shan't be able to see to catch them in the dark. But we'll come first thing in the morning." The only thing for Captain Ward to do was to return and by this time the fire had done its worst. He then went back to Cricklade to say that the fire engine would not now be required. "Very good" said the obliging fireman, "but I'll come over all the same in the morning and assess the damage." The fire not only consumed the building and all its contents but the rumours also and as far as I know the mystery as to whether any communications had ever been made with the enemy has not been cleared up to this day.

The "North Meadow" at this time was one hundred acres in extent so it is no wonder the horses could not be found.

* * * *

St. Leonard's Church, Minety.

St. Leonard's Church

ST. LEONARD'S CHURCH, MINETY, is a very ancient building of stone, described as Early English Style, with traces of Perpendicular work. It now consists of chancel, nave of four bays and vestry with an embattled tower with pinnacles. At the beginning of this century it contained a peal of five bells which had been rehung in 1892.

There are memorial windows to the Rev. John Edwards, a former Vicar who died in 1886; also to the Perry Keene family and tablets to Charles Pleydell, dated 1704; Joseph Nott, 1705; Thomas Brown, 1726. Other memorials include a Brass to the Powlett family.

There are many tombstones in the churchyard to members of the Keene family who, during the latter part of the eighteenth century and throughout the greater part of the nineteenth were the principal land owners in the district. Colonel William Thomas Keene Perry-Keene, J.P., D.L., was the last known of the family to reside in Minety. He lived at Minety House.

The Church Register dates from the year 1663.

The nave of the church was re-roofed in 1884 at a cost of £400, the tower restored in 1892 and the chancel relaid in 1894.

In 1906 the tower was showing signs that it needed underpinning as the foundations were sinking. This meant much work inside the building as well. It was decided then to make various alterations to the interior.

During the excavations necessary for the underpinning of the tower, some very interesting relics were brought to light which proved that a church had existed on the sight for over a thousand years. Remains of an Anglo-Saxon cross were found and this can be seen on the sill beneath the west window. Also, to enable the work to proceed several ancient coffins had to be removed, one which was in a very good state of preservation—having been hewn out of a solid tree trunk. In order that this could be better preserved, at the instigation of the Bishop of the Diocese it was taken to Devizes Museum.

In the 1920's it became necessary to enlarge the burial ground. This was done by enclosing and consecrating a piece of ground adjoining the east side that according to the map of Minety printed in 1828 had at one time been Glebe land.

More recently the old oak frames in the belfry in which the bells were hung were found to be unsafe and an appeal was made to raise funds for the rehanging of the bells. The response was generous and as a result it was possible to put new bearings in an iron frame and to increase the number of bells to a peal of six. This was completed in 1958.

During the Civil Wars of the sixteen-forties the district was continually in dispute between Cromwell and the Royalists and scars and indents resulting from cannon shot can be seen in the stonework and buttresses on the outer west wall of the church. As recently as the nineteen-thirties when the nearby Elms Farm was occupied by the Cole family, a cache or jar of flints of the type used in the old flint lock muskets of that time was uncovered there. One of these I have in my possession.

One stone in the churchyard is worthy of mention. It stands by the path to the south of the chancel. The inscription reads:—

In Loving Memory
of
GEORGE ANDREWS
who died Jan. 26th 1888 aged 83 years
He served 32 years in the 1st Life Guards
Entering as a Private he, by merit, rose
to be Captain
"Behold, God is my Salvation. I will
Trust and Be Not Afraid"
This was erected by his sorrowing Grandchildren

I have in my possession his Military Text Book entitled "A Treatise of Military Discipline" in which is laid down and explained

"THE DUTY OF THE OFFICER AND SOLDIER"

This was printed in the year 1759, during the reign of George II and bought at an Auction Sale many years ago as a junk lot. It has his signature on the fly leaf.

Another inscription reads:—

In Memory Of
George Vizer of this Parish
Who died Feb. 9th 1867
Age 40 years
Also of Ann his Wife
Who died May 8th 1904
Age 77 years
Also of six of their children
Francis Isaac, Died May 8th 1867, Age 10 years
Sidney, Died Feb. 11th 1867, Age 6 years

Kate, Died Mar. 21st 1867, Age 8 years
Frederick Edward, Died Dec. 1st 1870, Age 8 years
And two who died in infancy

An Act of Parliament was passed in the year 1667 that shrouds should be made of none other than sheeps wool. Enforced in 1678. Repealed in 1814. First such burial is recorded as being at Minety Church.

I should mention here a few items worthy of note. Writing in the Church Magazine of January, 1907 the Vicar, then the Rev. T. A. Ludlow Hewett, remarks that through the local farmers voluntarily hauling the stone for the underpinning of the tower from Garsdon, expenses were greatly reduced. This was all done with horses and carts.

Twenty years later when the burial ground was enlarged the new boundary hedges had to be replanted with "quick" or white thorn from Messrs. John Jefferies & Sons of Cirencester. This was brought by motor lorry which is just one example of the revolutionary change that was taking place in methods of transport.

The hedge surrounding the new burial ground was planted by Mr. Charles Stratford, the village smith, and his assistant, Frederick Pennell. It was Mr. Stratford too, who made the two ornamental iron scrapers that stand one each side of the south porch.

To the right of the path leading to Hovington House stands a yew tree that was planted by Ruth Matthews more than eighty years ago. Alas, the huge elm trees that lined the church path to the green when I was a lad—some of them six and eight feet in diameter—have now almost entirely disappeared.

About the turn of the century, Hovington House was rebuilt by the late Mr. C. F. Moore (of the firm of Moore, Allen & Innocent, Auctioneers) and many local men were employed. One day the Vicar at that time, the Rev. Walter Butt, had been visitng the church and on coming outside heard loud cries of distress from over the wall where the work was in progress. Rushing to the wall and looking over he saw to his horror a man with a rope round his neck drawn over one of the scaffold planks, the other workmen apparently threatening to hang him. It turned out to be nothing but a practical joke on poor Nathan Hughes. What the Vicar's reactions were is not recorded in history. However, they were all soon happily back on the job.

The old register which dates from 1663 contains the names of several families still living in this neighbourhood including:—

John, Son of John and Annie Hawkins. Born 1664.
Phillip, Son of Phillip and Margaret Timbrell. Baptised November 9th, 1664.
Henry Pritchard, Born February 1673.
Bridget Westmacott, Daughter of Thomas and Roberta. Born February 1678.
Henry Howse, Son of William and Jane. Born 1679.
Sarah Cool. Born 1686.
Giles Read, Son of George and Katherine. Born October 30th 1688.
Waldron (from Ashton Keynes). Married 1693.
Mary Coole. Christened September 19th 1697.

There is also an entry:—
Elizabeth Pleydell. Born September 13th 1698.

The Roll of Honour which hangs in the vestry gives the names of no less than ninety-five men of this parish who served in the war of 1914-18 and is as follows:—

YOUR PRAYERS ARE ASKED FOR THOSE WHO HAVE GONE TO
SERVE OUR KING AND COUNTRY BY LAND AND
SEA AND AIR

OUR ROLL OF HONOUR   MINETY, WILTS.

Addis F.	Law Benjamin
Baker Charles	Law Cecil
Baker Frank	Law Fred
Barnes Fred	Law Percy
Barrett Frank	Manners Leonard
Barrett Charles	Messenger Arthur
Bateman John	Messenger William
Bateman Charles	Miles Phillip
Blake Robert	Miles Percy
Brown William	Miles Jack
Burdock Ernest	Morgan Charles
Burdock Arthur	Morse Joe
Cantor Thomas	Morse Edward
Clayton Cyril	Morse Cecil
Clayton Harold	Morse Albert
Clarke Arthur	Musty George
Cook Harry	Newport Fred
Cooper	Newport Archie
Cole Jack	Payne Albert
Cowell William	Pennell Tom
Davis George	Peer Walter
Davis Jesse	Peer Jack
Davis Herbert	Ponting Howard
Freeth George	Ponting Nelson
Garland George	Ratcliff George
Gouldsmith Cecil (Major)	Read Frank
Hartnell Robert	Read Fred
Hinder Frank	Read William G.
Hinder Jack	Read W. (King)
Hughes Fred	Read Oliver
Hughes Nathaniel	Read William R.
Hughes Alfred	Read Rowland
Hook Percy	Read Tom
James (Capt.)	Read Sydney
Jones Arthur	Reakes Fred
Jones William	Smart Heber
Jones Eli	Smart Tom
Jones Mark	Smith Charles
Jones Joe	Smith William
Keates Charles	Smith B.
Keates Frank	Sparrow J.
Ludlow Hewitt E. (General)	Stratford Charles
Ludlow Hewitt A. (Capt.)	Stratford Frank
Ludlow Hewitt C. (Lieut.)	Taylor Cecil
Taylor William	Walker Mark
Vizer William	Westmacott Samuel
Waldron Tom	Westmacott Robert
Waldron William	Williams Harry
Waldron Jack	Wood Albert
Waldron Jim	Woodward ****
Waldron Jack	Yells Harry

There is also a brass plate by the Lectern which gives the names of those who lost their lives, viz.

"In Honoured Memory of the Heroes of the Parish of Minety who laid down their Lives for the Honour and Liberty of the Country"

F. Barrett
E. Burdock
T. Cantor
J. Davies
G. Garland
P. Miles
J. Morse
F. Read
T. Smart
H. Smart
W. Vizer
1939-45
C. Waldron

Water Supplies

To the present generation water supply is no problem. Just turn the tap and there is fresh, clear water, unless as unfortunately sometimes happens the supply is shut off by the local authorities on account of there being a burst water pipe. The mains water supply in the Malmesbury Rural District was carried out in 1936-37 and owing to the nature of the subsoil in this area being mostly clay which causes the steel pipes to rust and decay from the outside, many domestic tragedies such as flooded kitchens and yards and carpets ruined have occurred as a result.

Before this mains water supply became available each and every dwelling had to provide its own water supply either from a running stream, a "drinking pit" dug close to the house and supplied by surface water or by sinking a well. Many of these still remain. In some instances the wells were placed adjacent to the next-door house—especially in the case of semi-detached dwellings. They were usually from ten to twenty feet deep, three or four feet in diameter and walled up with stone. Sometimes a rope and winding gear was fitted and sometimes a long crooked stick was used on which to hang the pail which was weighted at one side of the handle enabling it to tilt and fill with water. Some wells were fitted with the old bucket type of pump, one of which I believe can be seen at Park House Dairy, Purton, the home of Mr. Bruce Grimes.

Story of the Well

IT was about the year 1900 that I had my first near-disaster when my father was living at the Moor Farm. It was usual to drive the horse and trap to Cirencester occasionally for my father to attend the market and my mother to do the shopping. Knowing it would be better to leave the children behind, my elder sister and myself were dropped off at Cooles Farm where our Grandmother Manners lived. During the day they suddenly missed me; it was no doubt teatime as it would not be exactly like me to miss a meal. A search was soon organised when loud wailing was heard, proceeding it seemed from the "bowels of the earth." It appears I must have looked down the well, overbalanced and have fallen in. It was lucky for me that there was enough water in the bottom to save me from breaking my neck but not enough to drown me. It could have ended very differently and this book would never have been written.

Stile and Well at Eastcourt

STANDING by the drive into "Sunnyside," Eastcourt, the home of Mr. and Mrs. J. H. B. Savage, is what appears to be just an ordinary well built stone stile with

Unique Stone Stile at Eastcourt which conceals a deep well, exposed by removing the stepping stone.

wide stepping stones each side, the stile itself being also one wide plank stone. It gives access to what was once the village school, now closed, as are so many others, and recently demolished. On sliding off the stepping stone there is revealed a deep well of clear cool water which was undoubtedly, many years ago, the domestic water supply to the surrounding properties. The property is now owned by Major Pitman of Eastcourt House. Although this is the only one I have come across, there may be other similar stiles in the county.

Eastcourt House lies just outside the boundary of Braydon Forest which extended as far as Wootton Bassett, Vastern and Brinkworth on the south, Swillbrook and the Thames on the north, Cricklade and the River Ray on the east and Garsdon, Charlton, Eastcourt and Oaksey on the west and embraced at one time about fifteen thousand acres, including part of Flistridge Wood.

* * * *

Schools

THE ST. LEONARD'S SCHOOL was built in 1856, the year that the steamship "Great Eastern," designed by Isambard Brunel was launched.

At this time these schools were known as "national schools," receiving a grant from the government according to their proficiency. The full effect of the building of the railway had not then been felt. But as time was soon to show, it became necessary to build another school and in 1875 the Silver Street School was built and the village was being virtually divided in half. My father, being born in 1853, with other members of the family, must have been among the first pupils to attend. I believe they paid a penny or twopence a week but it was not until the

31

St. Leonard's School, Minety. Also Schoolhouse in foreground. Built in 1856.

"Education Act" of 1870 was passed that compulsory education was established and in 1902, under Mr. Balfour's ministry, control of the schools was given to the county councils.

Substantially built of local stone these schools might well have stood for nearly a thousand years but having served its purpose for one hundred years, the St. Leonard's School was closed down in 1969, the senior pupils being taken to Malmesbury while the juniors went to Silver Street.

Silver Street School, as in the twenties.

Now in 1970, to keep pace with the times, increasing population, and the reorganising of educational methods, it has been found necessary to build a large modern school opposite the Silver Street School where there will be accommodation for something like three hundred children. This will be known as a Church of England Controlled School, incorporating the original Silver Street School.

But to get back to my original story of the schools.

Owing to an increased population it was found necessary in 1898 to enlarge the Silver Street School and the small classroom was added.

At this time these Church of England schools had to be virtually self-supporting. The only positive income was an annual grant from the Education Authorities for the two schools of little over £100, Fee grants £50, Betton's Charity £10 and Dean and Chapter £5. There was also a Diocesan Grant which could be applied for in extreme circumstances but the only certain income was about £165 out of which teachers' salaries and necessary upkeep and repairs had to be paid, the vicar and managers having to raise the rest by voluntary subscriptions. The rebuilding put them in the position of having to advance £55, and altogether at the end of the year the total owing to them was about £100 to the Vicar and £30 to the church wardens.

My father was a church warden and school manager at this time. As the other church warden was going to be away from Minety at the time of the next managers' meeting he wrote to my father to ask him to be sure to attend and concluded by saying "Could you not make a 'whip round' among some of those interested in these matters?" to help pay off the debt. However, owing to the efforts of the vicar and managers these difficulties were apparently surmounted. In 1904 the "Voluntary Association of Managers of Church of England Schools" suggested the formation of a scheme for a Common Fund consisting of a General Fund and a Special Fund, the Special Fund to consist of "such portions of any Parliamentary Grants payable in respect of a period before the appointed day and not required to meet outstanding liabilities incurred before that day."

After the first world war the local managers opened a "Fund for Improvements and Necessary Repairs" to the two schools as this had been waived during the war and the schools had become dilapidated. Unless this was attended to, the managers were in the unfortunate position of facing the alternative of having their school buildings confiscated by the Education Authorities and new buildings erected, the whole cost of which would fall on the rates.

It was estimated that £120 would meet the requirements of the Education Authorities and a fund was opened for this purpose. The situation was again saved by the generosity of local inhabitants.

Vast changes have taken place during the last fifty years. While the County Education Authority are responsible for the administration of the schools the cost now falls on the ratepayers. Of all the services now provided by the County Council for Wiltshire, education is the greatest expense. Out of a general rate of eleven shillings and sixpence in the pound for 1970-71, one shilling and ninepence is required for Education. These are the figures shown on the demand note for the second instalment due September 1970.

* * * *

Minety and Cirencester

MUCH has been written about Wiltshire by John Aubrey, William Cobbett in his *Rural Rides*, Leland and others of more recent times but few have much to say of this northern part of the county, one reason being perhaps that it has been tossed back and forth, sometimes being in Wiltshire and sometimes in the county of Gloucestershire.

Contrary to the belief of many is a fact that Minety belonged to the Abbey of Cirencester and not of Malmesbury. It is recorded that Richard I when fighting

Cotswold Stone Stile.

his Crusdades was prepared to sell anything to raise money to satisfy his creditors and that he sold the Manor of Cirencester which at that time included Minety, with its appurtenances, to the Abbot of Cirencester Abbey for one hundred pounds as money was then valued. This would include Taxes and Tithes and woe betide any man who was unfortunate enough to get into arrears.

At that time every large landowner, which included the Abbots, owned their own pit and gallows which were in great demand for Manorial offenders and were also available to smaller fry when occasion demanded. Such was the justice meted out.

In the first volume of *Gloucestershire Notes and Queries* a story is told about how, long before the Saxons invaded England, Cirencester was besieged by an African Prince who, after seven long years of unsuccessful siege, eventually set all his soldiers to catch sparrows to the tails of which were attached combustibles which were set alight and the birds released. They immediately flew under the eaves of thatched houses, catching them alight and so demoralising the inhabitants that the invaders were then able to storm and capture the town.

Cirencester was of great strategic importance even in the days of the Roman Occupation as it is here that the four great Roman Ways meet. Akeman Street from the south west, the Iknield Way, which runs east towards Oxford, Ermin Way from the north west towards Swindon and south east and also the Fosse Way running northward from Exeter to Lincoln.

Since the County Councils Act of 1888 the General Rate of Minety has been payable to Malmesbury Rural District Council, but the Rectorial Tithes were, until the Tithe Redemption Commission was formed, payable to the Dean and Chapter of Gloucester.

Since the Thames Valley Drainage Acts of 1871, 1874 and 1890, occupiers of land lying below a certain level were liable to a rate payable to the Thames Valley Drainage Commissioners, although the demand came from Cirencester, Minety was actually under the No. 1 (Cricklade) District Board. Certain land on the Moor Farm was liable for this rate and I still have a demand note dated 3rd June, 1929. particulars of which are as follows:—

No. 103.   Parish of Minety.
To Mr. H. Manners.   £   s.   d.
Rate at 1/– in the pound   2
The amount due must be paid on application to the Collector.

R. W. ELLETT, Clerk.

Rates in arrears for 28 days could be recovered by distress or by action at law, and furthermore the offender was penalised by not being entitled to vote at an election of members of the District Boards—rather severe penalties for default of payment of two pence!

*   *   *   *

The Hoar Stone

SAID to be the oldest piece of masonry on the banks of the Thames between its source and the sea.

Dates from Anglo-Saxon times and is mentioned in a grant of land by King Athelstan to Malmesbury Abbey.

Believed to be a boundary mark possibly between Malmesbury Abbey and Cirencester Abbey.

May have been hewn into a mounting block at a later date and used by travellers after letting their horses drink at the Thames.

The Hoar Stone.

This ancient monument stands on the south side of the Cirencester to Tetbury Road about three miles from Cirencester, and positioned as it is, it is passed un-noticed by thousands of motorists who actually drive within five or six yards of it.

It stands at the bottom of the batter where the road crosses over the old Canal almost opposite the old pumping house, so overgrown with nettles and brambles that it cannot be seen without stopping. A semi-circular wall has been built to protect it from being buried.

Cricklade

A FEW WORDS about Cricklade would not be out of place, especially as it was here that the V.W.H. Hunt kennelled the hounds for many years after moving from Faringdon, but I have more to say about this in another chapter.

Cricklade was, in the time of the Romans, a very important place, situated as it is, on the Thames and also more or less astride the old Roman road known as Ermine Street. An ancient poet wrote thus of Cricklade:—

Tower and turret crown your height
Thames lies babbling at your feet
Ghosts of Druids glide by night
Up and down your stony street.
Light men laugh and hurry past
Sentry of the Roman Way,
Shall you live to laugh the last
Wise old Cricklade, You or they?

For much of my Notes on Cricklade I am very fortunate in being able to refer to a book by Fred. S. Thacker, written in 1909, entitled *The Strippling Thames*, now unfortunately out of print. He had previously explored the Thames upstream by boat from Oxford to Thames Head, tying up at all places of interest and making a study of the surrounding countryside. He had access to sources of information which are not available to me.

Many of my notes are from this book which I found so interesting that I have read it through several times.

"Cricklade or old Cerriglad, one of the chiefest jewels of the Stripling Thames, visited by St. Augustine and forded here in 878 by Alfred the Great during his wars with GUTHRUN."

The old Chronicle says "Cnut the Dane sacked the town and cruelly harried the land around in 906. This year came King Cnute with a marine force of one hundred and sixty ships and caldorman Edric with him, over the Thames at Cricklade."

Town Bridge built in 1852, forty-four miles from Folly Bridge.

The old Irmin Way got obliterated some time north of the Bridge and the road was deflected from it due south through the town.

The bridge marked the jurisdiction of the Thames Conservancy which extended to the Teddington Wier.

Irmin Street once crossed the Thames half a mile below the present bridge.

The River Churn rises from two distinct well heads, Seven Springs, three miles south of Cheltenham and the other at higher altitude at Ullen Farm. The two brooks unite at Coberley. Seven Springs is ten miles further from the source than Thames Head and lies higher above sea level.

Tradition and sentiment continue to cherish Trewsbury Mead as the true fount of origin of the Thames.

Cricklade has two beautiful churches. St. Sampsons was built at the time of the first Pointed buildings, the tower dating about 1550. There are many interesting carvings both inside and outside the tower with its four pinnacles. The four aces, shears and sickles, the Peverels pepper garb and the Warwick Bear and ragged staff, the latter being over the south arch of the tower.

St. Mary's, which stands at the northern end of the town, has baresque Norman mouldings on the chancel arch said to have survived since about 1150. There is a beautiful old cross standing in both of the churchyards, the one at St. Mary's being in the better state of preservation. It is said that one of them originally stood in the street of the town and was removed to the churchyard when the old town hall was pulled down. This old "town house" stood in the centre of the street upon ten pillars, one of these old crosses standing in front of it.

An inscription on the south east side bore the date of its erection, 1569, which is also the date of the flying buttress.

It is discovered from documentary evidence that because Cricklade once succoured a queen in distress a native of the town may exhibit for sale without fee or

St. Sampson's, Cricklade.

licence, in the streets of any city of England and Wales, any such goods as are proper for merchandise. A Royal Charter is said to exist to this effect.

A story is told of how the inhabitants once stopped an undesirable Fair from setting up in the town by combining to occupy all the available space with stalls of their own produce.

Cricklade once contained a Royal Hunting Box now a Farmhouse known as Abingdon Court which was last occupied by Charles II. It is claimed to be the site of the first University ever established in England. The writer Ireland writes: "A Greek School was anciently founded here, or rather restored, by the learned Archbishop of Canterbury, Theodorus, and afterwards transferred to Oxford", adding that the town was remarkable only "by the mode by which they convey their dead for interment, which is by fastening the coffin in the front of a post chaise."

Jefferies, another writer, notes that when in conversation with a field labourer he was told that the water of a certain Tertoil Spring was said to be good for the healing of the eyes. The spring at Oak Barn, a couple of miles north of Cricklade was identified as the one with whose water St. Augustine, a year before his death cured the eyes of a blind man after his "conference at the Oak with a neighbouring British Bishop". The Oak was felled in about 1825 much against the wishes of a Lord St. German. The British Museum contains a document under the year 603 "Augustine called together Doctors and Bishops to commune in a place which to this day (1561) is called St. Augustine's Oak."

At one time there was a Russian Cannon at each end of the town, two being granted as the town returned two members to Parliament. One, Robert Jenner represented the town in the Long Parliament, dissolved in March 1660 after nearly twenty years. He also erected the Almshouses and planted at Marston Meysey Manor House one of the earliest Mulberry trees in the country, only cut down in the latter half of the last century.

Robert Canutus, "Robert of Cricklade" was Prior of the Anglo-Saxon Monastery of St. Frideswide when it was granted to the Norman Monks about 1158 by Adrian IV and after superintending the rebuilding of the Church he became Canon of Oxford.

In 1908 the Waylands estate had an average income of about £250 and supplied most of the funds for lighting and road repairs and thus greatly reduced the burden of the rates.

This estate largely arises from a bequest of Walter, Lord Hungerford, in 1449, for an annual Mass for the good of his soul to be said in the Hungerford, or Our Lady Chapel of St. Sampsons. It was diverted in 1566 by order of the Lord Chancellor towards the maintenance and lighting of the roads.

(1908) The property from which the income arises is situated in various parts of Cricklade and Chelworth, and consists of Orchards, Closes and Cottages.

The income is now paid over to the Rural District Councils in reduction of Rates, except for an annual sum of £50 for lighting.

This appears to be one of the rare instances of the use of these diverted Charity Moneys.

Another interesting Charity was devised by Charles I in the tenth year of his reign, which would be about 1635, the Braden Forest being then in the course of disafforestation. The King appointed that 100 acres of its area were to go to the poor of Cricklade and Chelworth for ever.

Thacker says, speaking of St. Sampsons, that "built into the North Porch is some tenth century sculpture: Perhaps an evidence of the existance of a Church here from that date of the Charities, another Hungerford Charity left by Sir Anthony and Dame Jane his wife in 1642, to provide annually fourteen upper coats or garments of cloth, on the left sleeves were to be 'set in red cloth the letters A.H.I.' " In 1908 the clothes were still given away, but the marking with the initials had been discontinued.

The free school provided for in 1651 by Robert Jenner was destined "only for the teaching of Latin Scholars, and none other." Thacker says, "The school still stands, a substantial house next to the Churchyard with a stone over the porch inscribed, 'This school was erected and 20 yearly settled on the Master by the bounty of Robert Jenner, Esq. AD 1652.' It was long used as a poorhouse until about 1840, then restored to its proper use, though they 'jonahed' the latin."

William Cobbett was in the town in 1821 and wrote in his *Rural Rides* with his usual savage indignation of what he saw—"I slept at a dairy farmhouse at Hannington". The day after he wrote this at Cirencester—"I passed through that villainous hole Cricklade about two hours ago and certainly more rascally looking place I never set my eyes on. The labourers look very poor, dwellings little better than pigbeds and their food not nearly equal to that of a pig. This Wiltshire is a horrible county." However, he was in a much better mood when he came that way again five years later and then wrote on hearing of the Thames and riding through it—(doesn't say where)—"it not being above four or five feet wide and not deeper than the knee of my horse, while the poor creatures that raise the abundant wheat and barley and cheese and mutton and beef are living on potatoes an accursed canal comes kindly through the Parish to convey all the good food to the Tax eaters in the Wen." (His genial and favourite epithet for London.)

Wootton Bassett

IN *Kelly's Directory* for 1885 Wootton Bassett is described as a market town and parish, formerly a borough governed by a Mayor, two Aldermen and twelve Capital Burgesses.

At the time of the Norman accession it was called Wodeton. About a century afterwards it became the property of the Bassetts from whom it received the adjunct to its name. By the Municipal Corporation Act of 1883 it would cease to be a Corporation, or the Incorporation would cease to exist after March, 1886.

Wootton Bassett was modern to the extent that it was lit by gas. Besides the monthly Cattle Market there were Fairs held on the sixth of April and the eleventh of October at which one hundred to one hundred and fifty agricultural servants were hired annually. As long ago as this Wootton Bassett boasted two Breweries, one listed as a "Steam Brewery" owned by Ernest Cauldwell, the other, still remembered by many, the "Beaufort Brewery" at that time in the hands of Howard Horsell. Needless to say there were many "beer retailers". There were also two Brickworks so that even in those days it would seem to have been a place of some importance.

Being essentially a dairying district and having the advantage of a railway line which put it within a few hours reach of London it was not to be wondered at that Wootton Bassett was chosen by some enterprising local business men as a convenient place to establish a Milk Depot. A business was started previous to the first World War named "The Dairy Supply Company" now renamed "Unigate Creameries Limited" at premises in the High Street which are now the egg department.

The milk collected was chiefly for the London market, transport being by road. Business expanded and it became necessary to build new premises nearer the railway. Eventually a special railway siding was brought to the factory. The milk was for many years transported in seventeen gallon churns (or eight barn gallons of two imperial gallons one pint as mentioned elsewhere).

Later bulk containers were used and on October 19th, 1927 history in this field was made when the first Bulk Milk Rail Tanker to run in this country left Wootton Bassett for London.

Owing to further expansion of the business it has been found necessary to reorganise the Company with depots at Wootton Bassett, Banbury, Moreton-in-the Marsh and North Kelworth, the headquarters being established at Wootton Bassett.

The transport section is responsible for a fleet of some seventy-five vehicles at Wootton Bassett alone and including "Unigate Dairy Sales" and "Devonshire Dairies (Swindon) Limited" they have to keep as many as one hundred and forty vehicles on the road.

The Company now finds employment for two hundred people according to season and the milk department is capable of handling fifty to sixty thousand gallons daily collected from approximately five hundred and eighty farms.

Besides handling bulk milk they also supply local retailers with milk already bottled.

The laboratory employs a qualified Analyst and a staff of seven locally recruited and trained girls on dairy hygiene and all milk is strictly tested for bacteria and keeping quality. Recently a new "Yoghourt" plant has been added, the most modern in the country with a potential output of one million pots per week.

Like nearly all of the small country market towns Wootton Bassett had to bow to the inevitable and lose its cattle market and Hiring Fair but with the advantage of such industries as the Milk Factory and Blanches Agricultural Machinery Works, to mention but two, Wootton Bassett has held its position as an important centre of industry.

Wootton Bassett, situated on the Southern fringe of Bradon Forest is noteworthy for its half-timbered restored Town Hall (1700) still standing proud and erect in the centre of the High Street on its 15 stone pillars. With stocks, a ducking stool and an ancient fire-engine, it is a great attraction to visitors.

There was a time when such visitors enjoyed sampling a well-known beverage, the product of the old "Beaufort Brewery", proprietors Marson, Owen and McNaught, who supplied the countryside for many miles around. In the year 1909 they were selling Beer to local farmers, a brew which no doubt satisfied the palate, at a price of four shillings and sixpence for a nine gallon cask. To prove it I have a receipted account.

Legend has it that at one time the local lock-up was under the Town Hall, known as the "Drunk Cell". If the old building could speak it would have much to tell. One story goes of a man who was unfortunate enough to be taken into custody for riotous behaviour. Being too drunk to appear before the Magistrate he was locked in the "Drunk Cell" until the next day. His friends visited him during the

Wootton Bassett Town Hall.

night, giving him as much more beer as he could take, by thrusting a long Church-warden pipe through the keyhole. With the pipe in the prisoner's mouth they poured the beer into the bowl. The consequence was that when the constable came for him the next morning he was in a worse state than when he was locked up.

Another tale goes of a man brought up on a similar charge after an overnight spree. When asked by the Mayor whether he pleaded "Guilty" or "Not Guilty" says he, "You knows yer Worship. You was just as drunk as I was," the Mayor having apparently been on the same caper. "Ah well" said his worship, "That's different. I'm the Mayor and I'm going to fine you five shillings."

It was said by some that this particular Justice of the Peace was none too good a scholar and a builder by trade, and that the Clerk in Office wished to shew him a document. Finding the Mayor up on some scaffolding he took the paper up the ladder for him to read. He took it from the Clerk and was earnestly scrutinising it when the clerk remarked "Excuse me sir, but you are holding it upside down". "That's no business of yours" retorted the Mayor, "I don't have to ask you, and I can hold it how I like."

Perhaps a pinch of salt could be taken but no doubt some of these stories are based on fact.

* * * *

Oaksey

THE parish of Oaksey, now pronounced as it is spelt, but for many years called "Woeksey" by the inhabitants (as Chelworth used to be known as "Chelloth"), lies to the north west of Minety which it adjoins, being separated by the Bradon Brook and Swillbrook, the latter forming part of the boundary of Bradon Forest. The road from Minety passes St. Leonard's Church, Tiddling Corner and the bridge at Oaksey Ford. In times of heavy rain this road is often under two or three feet of water and impassable. Before the railroad was built there was also a road leading from Minety Lower Moor across Home Farm, through fields, still known as "The Laines". Although a carriage way it was never metalled. From Minety Moor it crossed the road by Brandiers Farm, proceeded along through Ruddocks Lane, parallel to where the railway now runs, close by the site of an old cottage on Cooles Farm, once known as the "Owl's Nest" and last occupied by old John Randall about one hundred years ago. It eventually joined the present road at Tiddling Corner now renamed Lyngrove Farm, continuing across Oaksey Ford.

In 1863 the Oaksey Park Estate and Manor of Oaksey comprised some seven hundred and sixty-two acres. On 23rd July, 1863 it was offered for sale by auction at the "King's Head Inn", Cirencester. It contained several farms and holdings including in the First Part Woods in hand thirty nine acres, three roods, eleven poles, Woodfalls Farm 94a. 0r. 0p., Street Farm 99a. 3r. 4p., Sodam Farm 96a. 0r. 18p., and about twenty small tenements totalling 12a. 1r., 18p., about thirty "Incroachments from the Waste" totalling 1a. 0r. 11p. and five Lifeholds of 0a. 3r. 34 perches.

Oaksey Old Manor, or The Mansion, now demolished.

Of the Second Part, Oaksey Park Mansion House, Flistridge Wood and other lands and plantations of approximately 43a. 2r. 4p. at that time let to Mr. William Morse until February 1st, 1864. The Park Farm in the occupation of Mrs. Margaret Hiscock, containing approximately 271a. 1r. 27p. was let at a rental of £530 per annum. Oakwell Farm of 50a. 2r. 6p. and other small pieces of land 52a. 3r. 0p. or thereabouts.

In the "Summary of Particulars" 56a. 3r. 23 perches are shewn as situate in Crudwell. This comprised the Mansion House and Park Farm, the total acreage being seven hundred and sixty-two acres, one rood twenty perches and the total rents being £1549–14–7d. The estimated value of the property not let was £170 making the annual value £1719–14–7d.

The estate was subject to the following charges:—

	£	s.	d.
Moiety of the Fee Farm Rent payable to the Earl of Ilchester	20	7	5
Apportioned Land Tax in Oaksey	11	6	4
As to the Second Part.			
Moiety of Fee Farm Rent	20	7	5
Apportioned Land Tax in Oaksey	8	18	4
Land Tax in Crudwell	2	8	0
Annual payment to the Rector of Oaksey	1	5	0

I am indebted to Mr. Percy Hawkins for allowing me to take these figures from a copy of the "Particulars of Sale" published at the time. The Auctioneer was Mr.

John Holland. Mr. Hawkins' ancestors owned property in Oaksey for many years and I understand it was they who built Oaksey Moor Farm which has now been demolished.

The Church of All Saints is of thirteenth century origin with fourteenth and fifteenth century additions and some Norman work. There is a Perpendicular cleristory but no north aisle. The large medieval wall paintings of Christ of the Trades and of St. Christopher were uncovered in 1933.

One of the stained glass windows appears to be composed of a mosaic pattern. It is believed that many years ago the original window was blown out by a violent storm and that two elderly ladies of the parish gathered up the fragments of glass which were pieced together to make the present window.

*　　*　　*　　*

Watkins Corner

IN the village (or hamlet) of Purton Stoke which lies well within the area covered by Bradon Forest, there took place one of the last public hangings in this county. This was in the year eighteen hundred and nineteen. It is said to have taken place close to the roadside on Haxmoor Farm. The place is still called Watkins Corner and is between Purton and Purton Stoke on the Cricklade Road.

Watkins Corner, Purton Stoke.

There are people living in Minety today whose great-grandparent witnessed the gruesome event but over the years the story has become somewhat distorted and told in many different ways. One version is that Watkins killed a boy who was working in an allotment and stole his dinner. Another went on to describe how, after the execution, a stake was driven through his body which grew into a tree. Some say his heart was buried beneath the road. I have been told, however, on fairly reliable authority, that his body was handed over to a Surgeon at Cricklade for medical research.

At one time there was a number of large trees on this corner and it was customary in some places to hang the miscreant on the nearest suitable tree which is said to have been the case here, although a scaffold was erected which, after having served its purpose, was taken down and used in the erection of farm buildings at Purton Pry.

What should however clear up the story in the minds of those who would like to know the true facts are given in the following account from a newspaper published at the time and now in Devizes Museum.

"At about 9–30 p.m. on the evening of 7th May 1819 the body of a man was found lying in the road between Purton and Purton Stoke, having been shot through the chest. The dead man was Stephen Rodway, a coal merchant who lived at Cricklade and he had been returning from a business visit to Wootton Bassett. He had been robbed of all his money except for a few halfpence. Robert Watkins, an unemployed labourer from Wootton Bassett, was arrested for the crime and sent for trial at the summer assizes at Salisbury. The case was heard on Wednesday 28th July 1819 when he was found guilty of murder and sentenced to be hanged on the spot where the crime was committed.

"On Friday 30th July he was removed from Fisherton gaol, Salisbury to a place called Moor-Stones near Purton Stoke where a scaffold and gallows had been erected. The spot is commonly supposed to be where the road to Purton Stoke takes a sharp left hand bend which is now known as Watkins Corner. He was repeatedly pressed to confess his guilt but he continued to deny that he had taken any part in the murder. Even on the scaffold he remained composed and at his own request read aloud the 108th Psalm. In spite of the short notice a large crowd had gathered in the fields around this corner which was estimated to be between 10,000 and 15,000 people. They were well behaved but two hundred special constables had been sworn in for the occasion in case of trouble.

"Almost at the moment that he was hanged a violent thunderstorm broke overhead and raged for half an hour, after which the crowd dispersed quietly."

Ref. *The Times*, London,
Saturday 31st July 1819.
Tuesday 3rd August 1819.

CHAPTER THREE

From place to place

Flint Roads

IT is not generally realised that until well into the twentieth century roads consisted mainly of flint, gravel or sometimes what was known as "ballast" which was burnt clay. Fires were started, either wood and clay and earth was thrown on, and once a good hot core was obtained this would burn for a considerable time producing red cinders. This was raked away and more clay fed on and many lanes and drives through woods were made with this material. Often during road works this can still be seen. All roads at that time were "water bound." The first serious efforts at road making were made by wheeling the flints from heaps placed on the roadside on wheelbarrows, other men using shovels spreading the material evenly. A water cart was then drawn over the surface spraying water and this was followed by the steamroller, a huge affair with wheels six feet high and weighing several tons, the roller and water cart going over it alternately until the surface appeared to be satisfactory. I can still picture the gigantic steamroller with a prancing horse motif and "INVICTA" painted underneath.

There was still a long time to go before we had the "tarred" or macadam roads which followed.

After the flints, blue rock stone became available owing to the fact that it could be brought by rail. This was hauled from the railway stations by local farmers with horses and carts, some farmers specialising in this. Arthur Webb, who farmed at "Big Elm Farm," Charlton, was one of these. He had four or five strapping sons and could provide a good horse and cart for each of them. I believe they earned about half-a-crown a load. One of these sons, Frank Webb, now retired, nearly eighty years of age and living at South Cerney told me that he can remember when they have had as many as fifty truck loads of stone at Minety Station waiting to be moved. These stones were often straight from the quarries and weighed up to nearly half-a-hundredweight each and after they had been carted to the section of road where they were required they all had to be broken up with stone hammers by hand. The "stonebreaker" was equipped with a small hammer and a sledge-type hammer with which he attacked them first to reduce them in size. He then sat on a sack or on his coat, legs apart, breaking them down with the small hammer until they would pass through a 3in. guage which the road surveyor brought. I believe they were paid at the rate of 1/6d. per cubic yard, though many claimed that it should have been 2/-.

This was dangerous work resulting in smashed fingers and many a man lost an eye from splinters of stone, but later most of them wore metal eye protectors with small slits to see through—quite probably compulsory.

There have been many changes since those days.

It has always been the general practice, or at least since the use of the stage coach, to signpost the most important roads, milestones either of stone, iron or wood giving the distance, in the case of stage coach routes, from Hyde Park Corner, this being the termination of the run. Signposts giving direction with "handposts" at turnings and crossroads, etc., were as a general rule erected on a mound of green in the centre of the road, and in the case of crossroads, four-finger posts with names of the nearest village or town painted in black letters on a white ground.

Webb's team of stone carts.

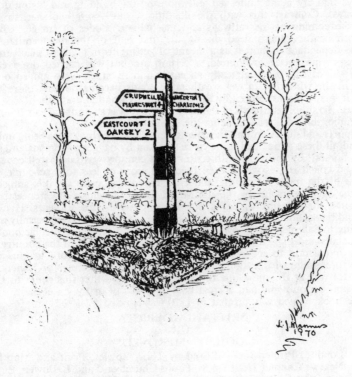

Sign Post at Murcott. One of the last to be left standing on turf in the centre of the highway. Map. ref. ST.965916.

These signposts were usually seven or eight feet high, but with the advent of the motor car it was found that by the time you were close enough to read the sign, the headlights of the car were focussed several feet too low and in order to read the sign it was necessary to stop the car, walk across the road and strike a match. So to overcome this drawback, the posts were cut down to about five feet in height.

One once-familiar sight in every town and village was the "Public Notice Board." These were four or five feet square and erected in prominent positions at the roadsides at such points as road junctions, bolted to posts at a convenient height for the "billposter" who was constantly going round the village or town sticking up public notices, police notices, "man wanted," "for sale" or perhaps advertisements. Walls of buildings abutting on to the highway were often rented by a particular party for this purpose in which case no-one else was permitted to use it. Where a property owner objected to the posting of notices there would be the old familiar sign "Stick No Bills." Of course there were the usual practical jokers so that the sign read "Stick Bills" or "Stick On Bills." It was also not unusual to find that a signpost on a crossroads had been worked loose in the ground and given a quarter turn so that each finger was pointing in the wrong direction with disastrous results for the unfortunate traveller who did not know the way.

WE in this twentieth century are fortunate, or the majority are, that we can travel from place to place in a car or coach entirely protected from the weather, on metalled highways that are being improved still more by the building and laying down of motorways. Contrast this with the conditions our forefathers had to endure before the coming of the railways and mechanised modes of travel. Until the eighteenth century and indeed during the first half of the nineteenth century, man was dependent on horses as a means of getting from place to place and also for transporting goods. Admitted, a certain amount was carried on rivers and later by the canals, but practically all cattle and livestock were moved on foot, so that in the winter or in wet weather the roads became nothing more than a morass in many places, especially those leading to London and other large towns and cities. To supply the needs of the butchers there was a continual trek of one-way cattle traffic, their destination being the slaughter house.

At ports and docks around the country merchandise ships were being unloaded daily and all these goods had to be carried inland by baggage waggons and strings of pack horses. By the eighteenth century this country was fairly well covered by recognised coach routes which even then ran more or less to a schedule.

One of the most interesting and comprehensive books on this subject was lent to me a few years ago by the late Mr. H. St. G. Rawlings of Cirencester, with whom I had the pleasure of doing business for more than 40 years. His collection of old books and maps would have been the envy of anyone historically minded or wishing to enlarge their knowledge in this direction. This pariticular book gave all the details and diagrams of all the principle coach routes in the country. Particularly interesting to me was the one from Bristol to Oxford as this passed through three miles of "Bradon Forest" and the southern fringe of Minety.

Bristol was at this time one of our chief ports so that this route to Oxford and beyond undoubtedly had a great deal of traffic of many varieties.

The book, which was printed in 1720 was entitled:

"BRITTANIA DEPICTA
OR
OGILBY IMPROVED"

London, Printed for and Sold by Thos. Bowles, Print and Map Setter, Next ye Chapter House in St. Paul's Churchyard and E. Bowen, Engraver and Print Seller (Setter?) Near ye Stairs in St. Katherine's.
1720"

The Bristol — Oxford Route is as follows: BRISTOL, STAPLETON, MANGRESFIELD, PULCHER, HINTON, TORMANTON WARREN, LUCKINGTON, FOXLEY, MALMESBURY, MILBURN, GUERSDEN, BRADEN FOREST, PURTON COMMON, PURTON, BLUNSDON, COLESHILL, FARINGDON, KINGSTON BAPTIST, FIFIELD, OXFORD

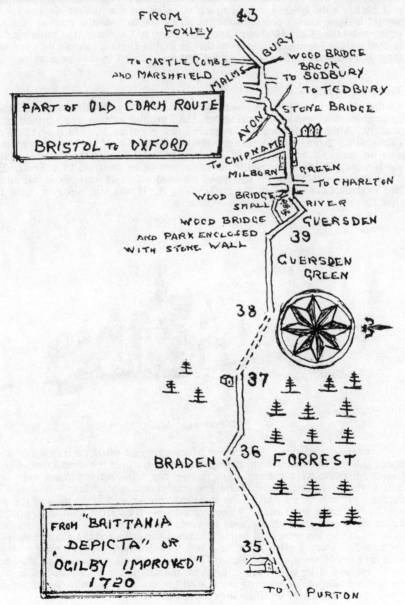

47

At this time the coach routes did not always follow what we today look on as the obvious route. The road from Malmesbury, it will be noticed, passes Braydon Manor from Garsdon, thence to Purton and Blunsdon, not through Charlton and Stonehill. In fact, according to the survey of 1773 by Andrews and Dury, the Charlton, Minety to Leigh road stopped at the "Three Horse Shoes" cross roads where it branches south to Duchy Rag on the Wootton Bassett road and north to the Swan Lane Turnpike at Leigh on the Ashton Keynes road. I should imagine that it crossed over the Cricklade to Swindon road at Blunsdon, possibly by the "Cold Harbour" and from there to Oxford by the same road that is used today. My illustration from the "Brittania Depicta" shows the road taken from Malmesbury to Blunsdon, so beyond that point I cannot be positive.

Turnpike System

As the old haphazard way of keeping up the highways by the local landowners and commoners was so unsatisfactory, the Turnpike system was adopted in this country. Although the word "Turnpike" first occurred in 1678 it was not until 1706 that the general system was introduced. By an Act of 1663 tolls were chargeable on certain roads leading to London, but in 1706, by the General System, roads were divided into sections, each section being assigned to a Trust. Each Trust was responsible for the upkeep of the road within its section and was authorised to collect charges from the traffic using it. It was not, however, until 1727 that Turnpikes were established in Wiltshire.

Old Pikehouse, Minety.

Charges varied from one district to another and often the paying of a toll at one gate might free you from paying at the next if within the same Trust. Certain classes of traffic were exempt from paying any toll. Among these were mail, troops, their transport, agricultural implements and pedestrians. Avoiding the payment of taxes is not new to the twentieth century and in the days of the turnpikes many ruses were used. Whenever possible the crafty road user would go across fields and through by-lanes to avoid paying the toll. Some of the well-mounted horsemen were said to have jumped the gates for the same reason and got away. A story I often heard as a boy was that perhaps on a market day or after an evening spent at the "Pig and Whistle" or some other such public house, the driver would be either drunk or tired and fall asleep in the bed of his cart, the horse would amble on until it came to the toll gate where it would patiently stand until morning or until the unfortunate driver awoke.

Even the turnpike system was not altogether satisfactory and fell into abuse when the railways came into being, carrying passengers, so that the revenue from the coaches dropped considerably. Later when the railways started carrying the complete coaches similar to the "container" system now in the process of being brought in, this spelt doom to the turnpike road. It was not until the "County Councils Act" of 1888, when the upkeep of the roads was taken over by local authorities that the problem was brought under control.

Although the "general turnpike system" has been out of use for close on one hundred years there are still some cases where tolls have to be paid, one of the more recent instances being the new Severn Suspension Bridge. There are a few others such as ferries, etc., but they are the exception rather than the rule.

Many of the old pike houses still remain in a good state of repair and housing families. Many have been demolished, some even during my lifetime. Some of the old notice boards giving complete lists of toll charges are still to be seen in museums over the country, including one at Malmesbury being the original board from "Charlton Street Gate" which is in a very good state of preservation with the lettering and figures clearly visible.

While Eastcourt Gate House has gradually deteriorated, one part with the old fireplace walled in still remains and is now used as a bus shelter, a roof one storey high having been fitted.

Eastcourt Pike House (demolished 1971). Map ref. ST.977926.

From Eastcourt to Minety the road passed through Flistridge Wood, Upper Minety, past the Fishpond to Silver Street School, there turning right to Minety Pike on the Malmesbury to Cricklade cross roads. This Minety turnpike was described on the Tollboard as the "Seven Bridges Gate" and was administered by the Malmesbury District Trust, the clerk being one Ino Heath. When the tolls were taken off this road the board was taken down and used as a coalhouse door.

Although suffering much from exposure to weather, not to be wondered at after a period of some ninety years, I was able to salvage it through the generosity of Mrs. Eli Jones who owns the house and has lived there for more than half a century and who kindly allowed me to take it in exchange for another door to take its place. I only regret I was unable to pluck up the courage to ask for it thirty years earlier when Mrs. Jones would have been just as willing to part with it. Much of the lettering has disappeared, but all is not lost as I have been able to obtain from Mr. Rathbone, Chief Archivist to the Wilts. County Council at Trowbridge, a complete list of tolls authorised by the trustees for this district of road, and am now in the course of restoring it as near as possible to its original form.

Duchy Rag Pikehouse on Braydon to Ashton Keynes Road at Black Dog Bridge. Map ref. SU.052903. Black Dog Bridge. Ref. SU.052899.

Copy of letter dated 29th July, 1969 from the County Archivist, Town Hall, Trowbridge.

Dear Sir,

MALMESBURY TURNPIKE TRUST

Your board with details of tolls must have belonged to the turnpike road which runs from Malmesbury to Highworth, passing through Charlton, Cricklade and Blunsdon St. Andrew. This part of the Malmesbury group of roads, which were first turnpiked in 1755-6.

We have here a copy of the third act relating to this trust, 1777-8, 18 Geo. 111, c. 114. The scale of charges laid down in this act is as follows:—

"For every Horse, Mare, Gelding, Mule, Ass, Ox, Bullock or other beast of draught, drawing in any carriage,
The sum of six pence.
For every Horse, Mare, Gelding, Mule or Ass, not drawing,
The sum of two pence.
For every drove of Oxen, Cows or Neat Cattle, twenty pence per score, and so in proportion for any greater or less number.
For every drove of Calves, Hogs, Sheep or Lambs, Ten pence per score, and so in proportion for any greater or less number."

The Toll was only payable once in each day, i.e. a return journey before midnight was free. There were some exemptions, including local agricultural and road-mending vehicles.

Yours faithfully,
(Signed) Maurice G. Rathbone
County Archivist

L. J. Manners, Esq.,
Moorfield,
Minety,
Malmesbury,
Wilts.

Pike House, Collins Gate, Purton, Wilts.

A pikehouse at Purton now occupied by Mr. and Mrs. Wesley West is described as "Collins Lane Gate." The toll charges are inscribed on the wall of the house and are in a very good state of preservation.

COLLINS LANE GATE

Wagons or Carts with 9in. or 6in. Wheel	5½d.
,, ,, 4in. or less than 6in.	5d.
,, ,, less than 4½in.	6d.
Drawn by one horse, one horse only......	6d.
Coaches, Chariots, Chaises, Hearses, Gigs, Chaps (Traps)	4½d.
Every Horse, Mule or Ass adrawing	5½d.
Oxen, Goats, Cattle, per score	10d.
Calves, Sheep, Lamb or Pigs, per score	5d.
Two or more neat cattle drawing pay as one Horse	

All tickets delivered at this gate frees Cricklade Dance, Broad Leaze, King's Hill, Packhorse, Purton Poor Street and Liddiards Marsh Gate.

Also shall all cases when any waggon or cart shall descend this hill in this District or Road will either of them, Chain Locked or Skid-pan and Slipper shall be used to the bottom of such, wheel dragging the whole time of its being locked.

By order of the Trustees,

J. Pratt, Clerk

Descending hill with skid pan or "Drag Shoe" locking rear wheel to act as brake.

Another such Pike house still exists on the main road between Cheltenham and Evesham with an inscription which reads in part:—

TOLLS 1838
TO BE TAKEN AT THIS GATE

For every horse, mule or ass not drawing .... 2d.

For every horse, mule or ass or other beast of draught drawing any coach, chaise phaeton, curriel, gig or waggon .... 6d.

For every drove of oxen, cows and new cattle per score ...... 5d.

For every drove of pigs, calves, sheep or lambs per score 5d.

CHARLTON STREET GATE

A table of the tolls to be taken at this gate by Order of the Trustees of this District of Road.

For every Horse, Mule, Ass, Oxe or other beast drawing any Carriage having the fellies of the wheel thereof less

52

breadth or gauge than four and a half inches from side to
side at the bottoms or soles there of the sum of .... 6d.
For every Horse, Mule, Ass, Oxe or other Beast drawing any
Carriage having the fellies of the wheels thereof the breadth
or gauge of four and a half inches and less than six inches
at the bottom or soles thereof, the sum of .... 5d.
For every Horse, Mule, Ass, Oxe or other Beast drawing
any carriage having the fellies of the wheels thereof the
breadth or gauge of six inches or upwards at the bottoms
or soles thereof, the sum of .... 4d.
For every Horse, Mule or Ass, laden or unladen and not
drawing, the sum of .... 1d.
For every Dog drawing any wain, truck, cart or other
carriage, the sum of .... 1d.
For every drove of Oxen, Cows or neat cattle, per score
and so in proportion for any greater or less number, the
sum of .... 1/8d.
and for every Drove of Calves, Hogs, Sheep or Lambs
per score and so in proportion for any greater or less number,
the sum of .... 10d.

Paying Toll at this Gate frees Whitchurch Gate or Perry Green, Charlton
Moor, Charlton Common and Five Lane Gates.

JNo. Heath, Clerk

Charlton Street, Turnpike House.

* * * *

Railways

MANY STORIES worth putting on record have been handed down from the days
before the railways came through the village in about 1838-41, and Isambard
Kingdom Brunel, who was engineering the project, was often seen riding round
on horseback. This was the most revolutionary, useful and beneficiary change
that had ever taken place until that time, making it possible to travel in comfort
at a reasonable cost. The railway line running north-west by what is known as
London Road, through the Lower Moor between Cooles and Brandiers Farms,
both of which are marked on the Survey map of 1773 made by John Andrews and
Andrew Dury, cut the village virtually in half. The railway station was at the
extreme east of the village and the church almost the extreme west, there being

two miles between, so that over the last one and a half centuries Minety has gradually developed around the station end to the neglect until recently of the old original village centre and green which still exists.

There lived in Church Path Cottage until the early part of this century an old Mrs. Pretty, who could remember her mother carrying her down to the level crossing near Brandiers Farm to watch the first train pass over. I have a photograph of her and other members of her family standing by their cottage gate from the road entrance showing part of the old Church Farm House which was demolished at the turn of the century. The stone was used to help build what is now known as Hovington House, originally known as "Church Farm" and then owned by the late Fred Moore, founder of the firm of Moore, Allen and Innocent, which is still flourishing.

Type of Stile erected by the Railway Company.

This is typical of the stiles erected by the Railway Company, usually of sawn timber. At the beginning of the century there were nine points in the parish of Minety, including the Level Crossing and footway at Brandiers and the road bridge at Minety Station, where the railway could be crossed. There were four footpaths across, two road bridges *under* and the road bridge *over* on the Malmesbury—Cricklade Road.

During the first decade of this century because of the number of school children using the Sambourne footway and the considerable amount of fast traffic and shunting into the Minety sidings which reached beyond the Sambourne footpath, the Company erected an iron footbridge for safety reasons. I well remember this bridge being put up when I was a small boy and going during the school dinner break with a number of other boys to inspect the work. On one occasion, before the footboards had been fitted, I remember climbing up and attempting to cross over the line on a scaffold plank, when a goods locomotive and train happened to pass underneath. What with noise, smoke, and red hot cinders I should have fallen with fright if one of the men had not held on to me.

Transport Development during the Twentieth Century—First Aeroplanes

Among the wonderful scientific and mechanical achievements of the twentieth century the advancement in methods of travel have been one of the most useful contributions to the benefit of mankind. On land, in the air, on the water and under the sea, countless new theories have been advanced and put into practice. In the air, the invention of "heavier than air" type, has in my opinion shown the most progress of all during my lifetime. I well remember the efforts of the Wright Brothers who were pioneers in the field of aviation and the encouragement given by the *Daily Mail* in offering huge prizes, first for a circular flight of a given distance and then increasing the prize money as machines improved. A most exciting event was the attempt on the first Channel crossing when Englishman Hubert Latham failed by a few yards, coming down in shallow water just off the English shore and the Frenchman, M. Bleriot, took to the air before Latham could make another attempt, thus robbing him of the honour.

A model of his machine, a monoplane, was suspended high overhead in the Crystal Palace. I saw it there during a visit in 1910. This tremendous structure built on a strong framework and covered entirely with glass and containing many very interesting exhibits, tableaux of scenes and natives of nearly every country of the world and one of the best roller skating rinks in the country, was completely destroyed by fire some years later. This great Exhibition had attracted many thousands of visitors. It was a landmark for miles around, especially when illuminated at night and was sadly missed.

The first time I saw an aeroplane in flight was an experience that I shall never forget. It was in the summer of 1911. We were haymaking in a field situated at the far extremity of the farm, the field sloping in a northerly direction and bounded by the high hedges of the Rudge Lane. At first we heard what seemed like some sort of machinery approaching from behind the hedges. My first thought was that it was a traction engine labouring up the lane, the steam-powered traction engines of that time being the only kind of machinery I could think of. Suddenly there appeared over the top of the hedge and coming directly towards us at fifty to a hundred feet up was what I thought must be a hay elevator being airborne as though caught up in some whirlwind or supernatural power. The speed was very low and the noise was terrfic and it was not until it had passed over us and we could see the pilot sitting exposed amongst the struts and stays that we were able to grasp the fact that we had actually been watching one of the first "heavier than air" flying machines. That evening when we were back in the house the sound was heard again and everyone rushed out of the house to see it pass over. In the excitement my young sister fell and gashed her forehead against a sharp corner of a wall and still bears the scar. This was not the only near tragic incident caused by this historic event. My Grandmother Manners at Cooles Farm had given us children a donkey and small Governess car which was as big a treat as she could possibly have given us. We never tired of either riding or driving it. But like most of its tribe it was extraordinarily obstinate and slow. Its coat was thick and heavy, almost as thick as a feather bed and no matter what stick was used to persuade it to get moving it was impossible to make it felt. Pulling, tugging and whacking had little effect, but directly its head was turned towards home away it went with a gallop.

We made our own harness, breast harness type, using an old girth for breast collar, pieces of rope for the traces, and one of our favourite games was to get an old milk pan such as those used in the dairy, flat round shallow pans with drop handles which were used for setting up the milk to be skimmed, milk fresh from the cow when as it cools the cream rises to the top. It is then taken off with a skimmer and put in a cream tin till "butter day" which is once or twice a week. The cream is put into the butter churn which is turned by hand until a large lump of unsalted butter separates itself from the whey or buttermilk. The buttermilk is fed to pigs.

To go back to my story, having hitched the donkey by means of the traces to the milk pan, two of us would coax, persuade or by some means entice the obstinate animal about half a mile or so along the road, until we decided we could get no further. We would then let go its head, scramble into the milk pan and the crafty old "moke" would immediately turn round and bolt for home as fast as he could put his feet to the ground while we hung on to the reins for our lives!

Luckily for us there were no motor vehicles on the roads and we could always be sure that as long as we could hang on we should eventually arrive home.

I am afraid I have rather gone off at a tangent and strayed from my story, but it so happened that at this time, what to us was a phenomenal event of seeing our first aeroplane in flight took place. My young brother was in the hayfield on the donkey's back. It is not necessary I am sure to remind you of the size of a donkey's ears, generously bestowed by nature, nearly a foot in length. Ample in size and equally sensitive. The donkey, likewise heard this strange vibrating noise, and after swinging its ears as though searching for a radar beam, it suddenly brought them to what that greatest statesman of all time would have described as the "V Sign," simultaneously turning tail and galloping off minus its rider, my brother having by this time found himself on the ground.

According to a report in the local press, the aeroplane had been on a flight from Netheravon to Cheltenham, and of course we were in the line of flight.

* * * *

Planes and Cars

LOOKING BACK to the turn of the century when the railways held sway and were regarded as the ultimate in luxury and speed it seems almost impossible to believe that within perhaps twenty years the whole aspect of travel would be revolutionised by the coming into general use of the motor car, motor cycle, motor coach, aeroplane and now the hovercraft.

The hovercraft is neither a boat nor an aircraft which reminds me of the words of a song that was very popular forty or fifty years ago entitled "It ain't gonna rain no mo." One verse proclaimed:—

> The Butterfly has wings of gold,
> The June bug has the same,
> The Bed-bug has no wings at all
> But it gets there just the same.

This, to me, just about sums up the hovercraft.

The following account of pioneer aviation was published In the *Church Monthly* of January, 1907:—

THE NEW FLYING MACHINES
MOTOR KITES AHOY!
by F. M. HOLMES

"Before long, it is said, mankind will be able to fly. The fairy carpet of the eastern tale will be a reality and persons will be whisked through the air with the rapidity of a bird on the wing. (After mentioning the three methods of flight, the Balloon, the Airship or Dirigible Balloon and thirdly the Aeroplane, the article goes on) and "planes" or lengths of light material are used, stretched over light poles and driven rapidly by a motor.

No doubt there is a great difference in the exact shape of these "planes" and the manner in which they are used, also in the kind of motor employed. Scores and perhaps hundreds of inventors are busy in all parts of the civillsed world trying experiments.

But the shapes adopted by M. Santos-Dumont in Paris and by Major F. S. Badén-Powell in one of his models in England, and said to be adopted by the Wright Brothers in Ohio, U.S.A. appear to be all more or less variations of an elongated box kite.

Imagine a long "box" of light material, some eighteen feet in extent

The new Flying Machines—Motor Kites ahoy!

by seven feet deep—the measurements of Santos-Dumont's machine — but having the two sides open, so that the wind blows freely through it.

The "box" thus offers scarcely any resistance to the wind, yet it is filled with air. M. Santos-Dumont employs two of these "boxes," one on either side of a light car, from which they slope slightly upward, and appear not unlike the wings of a large dragon fly's body, ending in another "box" which contains the rudder, while the propeller is fixed on the other side of the car.

With a machine like this on November 12th, 1906, a date we expect to become famous in aerial annals, the clever and daring young Brazilian aeronaut "flew" some seven hundred feet at the rate of about twenty-five miles an hour. He soon began to improve his machine by building, it is said, another with an even lighter motor, and possibly shorter wings.

The maintenance of a perfect equilibrium is one of the most important points.

Major F. S. Baden-Powell, who invented a man-lifting kite some years ago, uses in one of his models two long planes one above the other, with a space between, through which the wind blows, and a small square plane in front, and a fan-shaped tail behind.

He is in constant communication with the Brothers Wright, and believes their machine much resembles this model, except that the ends are not closed, and in one picture we have seen, the "tail" appears upright, answering the purpose of a rudder.

It is the motor which has apparently been giving Messrs. Wright so much trouble; it appears to be a petrol engine, and they have been endeavouring to perfect it so that it shall run quite smoothly and reliably. In fact, it is the use of a thoroughly suitable motor which seems to form one of the chief difficulties in "flying" together with the necessity of maintaining a perfect equilibrium.

Wright Brothers kept their apparatus as profound a secret as possible, hoping to sell it to the United States Government, and some reports indicate that they may have done so, and that the Government is to build an aerial fleet.

And so, propelled through the air on wings of a kite by an extraordinarily powerful but extremely light engine, Mankind is to fly! It has been the dream of ages. Man has long envied the birds, and now he seems about to rival their swift flight.

Above the tree tops he will soar, mayhap mingling with clouds and basking in the sun, and bowing to the swallows as he passes.

It is an extraordinary prospect, and should it come to pass, will prove another great triumph of perseverence and skill.

*   *   *   *

Little did writers of that day know of the tremendous progress that was to be made during the following fifty years, that it did indeed come to pass and that by the year 1969, by perseverance and skill, men were to actually land on the Moon.

IN what to me, as a child, seemed an age of wonders it is not surprising that my first encounter with a motor car is something that will always stand out in my memory. It was in about 1907 when I was ten years of age. The Scripture Inspector, a clergyman, was making his annual visit to the Silver Street School which was still administered as a church school. To the amazement of everyone that morning, what should draw up outside the school and come to a standstill outside the entrance, but a large grey, brass mounted, open top four-seater motor car with a uniformed chauffeur looking like a general, and sitting in the back seat, covered with a large leather rug was the Scripture Inspector. It was raining heavily at the time and naturally they were both very wet. After he had concluded his examination he was due to visit the St. Leonard's School, at what is now known as Upper Minety. Being new to this part of the country, neither the clergyman or the chauffeur knew the road to St. Leonard's, so our old schoolmaster, John Cox, possibly knowing my connections with St. Leonard's and he being the church organist and knowing me to be a regular attender at church with my parents, asked me if I would accompany them and show them the way, and they would bring me back on their return journey. I could scarcely believe that I was going to have a real ride in a motor car and needed no further persuasion.

The chauffeur had, meanwhile, been sitting in his seat all rugged up, but as the seats of the car were leather covered and buttoned, the seat where I would have to sit was covered with pools of water. So in order to avoid soaking my pants I was obliged to stand up and hang onto the dashboard fittings. With potholes in the road and the high pressure tyres the journey for me was a matter of having to hold on with all my might and main and try to keep my nose from coming too closely in contact with the windscreen.

Going over the "Hills" at what seemed to me to be a terrific speed could only be compared with riding on the "switchback" at a fair. Needless to say, I was the envy of all the children and that day a seed was planted within me that took root and gave me a sense of "mechanical mindedness." My whole future from that day onwards seemed to be centred around motors and machinery and I was drawn as a moth ls attracted by a flame, so when in my early twenties I set up in business with a friend of mine, Philip Miles, who had served through the war ln the "Royal Flying Corps," later to become the Royal Air Force. With very little capital but a large and generous amount of credit, we opened the first petrol fiillng station in Minety with car and motor cycle repair shop. We also purchased an old "Chevrolet" touring car with which we did hire work and a one-ton Ford truck for general haulage. I shall perhaps refer to this enterprise later.

*   *   *   *

Cycles and Motor Cycles

I still have a vague memory of the old "penny farthing" bicycle and especially one that lay on a heap of rubbish in the Sawyer's Hill Allotment for some years. I believe it was the property of old John Cantor who had either grown too old to ride the machine or else the machine was too old for him to ride. Anyway, eventually it disappeared along with a load of old iron.

Now, motor cycles we had heard about but so far had never seen, until round about 1907, when the Silver Street Post Office was situated and carried on in the house opposite the school house now known as "Triscombe." It was also a grocery and sweet shop and did very good business being so close to the school. Although much of the income came from pence, not pounds, there was a steady stream of children all the week after school with their coppers to spend and perhaps some groceries or stamps to buy and take home. Now Frederick Hinder, son of the village blacksmith, was also mechanical minded, had a bicycle and did small repairs, punctures, etc., this being a specialist job as bicycles were then new on the market and no one knew much about them. Most bicycles ran on solid rubber tyres which were very heavy and were secured to the rim by a kind of white cement which was sold in cakes. To fix the tyre the bicycle was turned over, wheels in the air, you then armed yourself with a red hot poker, lifted a section of the tyre from the rim, inserted pieces broken from the cake of cement and immediately laid the hot iron on the cement which melted like wax, and so on, rotating the wheel until you had been all round.

These tyres were very dangerous if they came unstuck as the weight on the bicycle caused them to stretch and the tyre in front would perhaps be three inches ahead of the wheel. If you then turned the handlebars too quickly the rim would run over the tyre which would become jammed in the forks and if it happened to be the front wheel it caused a somersault with the inevitable consequences. Cycling was not too luxurious a mode of travel then when the road surface was composed of flint, stones, some two or three inches in size and innumerable pot holes.

However, to go back to my story, Fred Hinder had a brother, also in the cycle business, and it was not long before Fred had acquired a motor cycle—second hand—and of course as he lived opposite the school it caused great excitement among the pupils. As near as I can remember it was belt driven from the engine shaft to a large pully in the rear wheel, the brake being a shoe which pulled against the inside of the pulley, foot operated.

The engine of this type of motor cycle was what was known as "fixed type," there being no gears or clutch so that you could not push the machine without having to push the engine over compression. They were usually fitted with an "exhaust lifter" mechanism which depressed the exhaust valve for starting purposes. The ignition was supplied by a celluloid 4-volt (?) battery attached to a frame, thence through a high tension coil to the plug which fired the engine if you were lucky.

The usual method of starting was to turn on the petrol, flood the carburettor, switch on ignition, depress the exhaust valve, push the machine along the road as fast as possible, release the exhaust with the throttle partly opened and directly the engine showed signs of life, leap into the saddle with a flying motion and trust to providence that you landed safely thereon. Some of the lighter models were fitted with pedals so that if you had strength enough you could pedal the machine until the engine took over. I have known this to be a most exasperating process and usually if you encountered a slight incline you would have to dismount and run alongside pushing to keep going. It was generally after a deal of tinkering that old Fred pushed off from the post office, past the school in the direction of Hornbury Hill where there is a moderate incline. Very soon the machine would begin losing power and come to a standstill while poor Fred would come back pushing it, go through the process of tinkering again and repeat the attempt.

No doubt he got away eventually but many were the trials and tribulations of those pioneer motor cyclists. Besides the exhausting business of having to dismount at every incline and run alongside, often before you had completed your journey you would find your battery used up and useless. Unless you had taken the precaution of carrying a spare the only thing to do was to take off the belt and either push or pedal to the nearest place where the battery could be recharged. The dynamo driven by the engine had not then been invented, neither was the magneto in general use. In those days there were so few mechanised vehicles on the road that the sound could always be recognised and you would know who was driving any motor that passed along the road even though you had not seen it. This was especially so in the case of motor cycles, four strokes and two strokes.

As the roads were surfaced with flint which was ground to a fine powdery sand by the iron tyred traps and carts so that it lay thick on the road; in dry weather there was always a huge cloud of dust following all motor vehicles which could be seen rising a mile away. The grass verges and hedges were white with dust and I well remember the unpleasantness of trimming these hedges which affected both eyes and lungs. In wet weather the dust became mud and the road men had to carry long scrapers to scrape it into heaps on the grass verge. This mud was then sold, probably by tender to be used as mortar for building after mixing with slaked lime. Wherever an old building is demolished the flints will be seen. Although it had been screened or put through a sieve there were always small flints in evidence.

As was only natural, one's great ambition in life seemed to be to own a motor of some description, depending on one's financial position. A fairly usable motor cycle could be bought, second hand, for from five to ten pounds, and by the time I was eighteen I had managed to amass this amount. I heard that Messrs. Bailey Bros. of Cirencester had a machine for sale. The doors of shops and businesses were not then locked at five to five-thirty but remained open to give a service at any time of day. So one evening, taking a friend with me, we went and examined the machine, neither of us knowing very much about mechanically propelled vehicles. We decided to have a gamble and I purchased it for £5. It was of about 1908-10 vintage to wit, five horsepower, four cylinder in-line engine, shaft drive via chain stay, direct from crankshaft to rear wheel. There were no gears or clutch so that to move the machine without the engine running it was necessary to push the engine over compression which was no easy task, and when the engine eventually took charge it was away like a flash of lightning and with the agility of a cat you had to leap into the saddle.

Unfortunately for us we were no experts in mechanics and I had to push the thing almost as far as I was able to ride it. Within a few weeks I was able to sell it at a loss of five shillings and purchase a belt driven "Singer" 1½ h.p., which was in very good condition. But as I had by this time qualified for a licence to drive on the highway and also attained military age, World War I being in progress, I was forced to make a choice and decided to get into uniform. Having had experience with horses I joined the Royal Field Artillery which had then been mechanised but was also equipped with horses—not only horses but Spanish mules as well. They taught me more than all my previous experience had done. I was soon to know the full meaning of the expression "could kick like a mule!"

Every morning, on first parade at 6-30 a.m., all the gunners were detailed to help the drivers with "stables" which meant brushing and cleaning the horses sponging their nostrils and docks until the drivers had put the "feeds" of chaff and oats, etc., each deposited in a carrier and stood on the long roadway which ran between two lines of horses, standing in open stables tail to tail.

When this was all ready the Sergeant would blow his whistle and each man immediately hung up his brush and curry comb and stood back by the "feed" placed ready for him. The bugler then blew one long blast which signified "feed," and before you could get anywhere near your horse there was pandemonium with horses and mules whinneying, bucking and kicking. Unless you were very quick and lucky you would find yourself sitting back in the gangway with an empty feed tin, its contents scattered all over the ground.

You never knew which horse you were going to have as each man at the rear dropped off opposite a horse as we were marched through the lines which may contain anything from twenty to forty horses in a row. On one occasion the man who had the stable just before mine had a large Spanish mule just about as wild as a tiger and as he was rushing in with the feed in his hands this mule just waited until the poor fellow got within range and then caught him on the head with both feet kicking him right out flat on his back. He was carried away on a stretcher and consequently missed the draft overseas. I heard afterwards that he was in hospital for six weeks and I am very doubtful if he ever fully recovered from his injuries. But for Providence it could have been me.

My prospects of enjoying the luxury of owning a motor cycle were now suddenly interrupted with other things to occupy both my time and my mind. But having an occasional few days leave in the winter of 1917 I decided to get the old machine out and visit relatives at Edge, near Stroud. Petrol was very difficult to get and so I tried running on paraffin. By strapping an oil tin with a tap to the side of my petrol tank and running an extra pipe to the carburetter I was able to put petrol in this small can for starting purposes and paraffin in the petrol tank. As soon as the engine warmed up I could switch off the petrol and turn on the paraffin. I found that my engine ran perfectly by this method apart from hill climbing. There was less power with using paraffin and also it tended to soot

61

the plugs. Nevertheless it answered the purpose although I cannot claim that it was strictly legal.

My trip to Edge also meant journeying over the Cotswolds, bad enough at the best of times with a single geared, belt driven 1½ h.p. motor cycle; but to crown it all, before I could start my return journey snow started to fall and by the time I was able to get going it was lying thick on the road. From Edge to Stroud the going was quite good as it was nearly all downhill but when it came to ascending the hill into the town I immediately ran into trouble of the first magnitude. The snow throwing up on to the driving belt caused it to slip so that there was absolutely no grip at all.

I could see that it was quite impossible to get home under such conditions. The only thing to do was to push the machine to Taylors, the nearest garage, walk to Stroud railway station and complete the journey by train, hoping at some future time to be able to go back and collect it.

The sequel to this was that some time after our adventure, my friend Phil Miles was home on leave from the R.A.F. and as my younger brother had by this time acquired an old belt driven, four horse-power "Triumph," they decided it would be a good opportunity to get my machine home. So they went to Stroud together on one machine. As the snow had all gone they were able to bring it back home where it was left in a back shed until the war ended. Then one of the things I had to do was to give the "bike" a look over and get it on the road again. Great was my disappointment when I found that through standing so long out of use the engine was stuck fast and it was only by filling the cylinder with paraffin and using brute force that I was able to get it moving.

However, as they say, "Nothing succeeds like success" I did eventually get it going and as one may well imagine I never again gave it the opportunity to seize up through lack of use.

Although by the commencement of the 1914-18 War cars and motor cycles were no uncommon sight, they had not really come within the reach of the ordinary citizen. Those who were fortunate enough to be the proud possessors of mechanical transport were mostly in the higher income bracket. The man in the street still rode a bicycle or drove a horse and trap. To the coming generation luxury travel was just around the corner and it was not long before second hand vehicles and motor cycles were on the market at prices varying from £2-10-0d. upwards and no Ministry of Transport Certificates were necessary.

Among others, H. O. King of Oxford was one of the first to see the way the demand for motor cycles was increasing. Having a coal business on the Canal Wharf and Oxford being a University city he was soon doing good business with second-hand motor cycles. Every available shed and lean-to that he could use contained an assortment of the machines of every description. Much advertising and a team of expert and fluent salesmen saw to the rest and youths and men from practically all over the country flocked there. You wanted a machine. He had it. You had a trial run if you were sufficiently safe to drive it, there were as a rule no guarantees and you just took a chance that you had picked a good one. I never kept count of the number of machines I bought from him, either for myself or for those who thought my judgement may be better than their own. Sometimes a purchase turned out to be a "pig in a poke" and before getting home with it the reason for its being on the market was discovered. It was not always the fault of the vendor if a machine failed to get home as many of the aspiring motor cyclists who bought them had little knowledge of mechanics. I remember many a time seeing some unfortunate individual sitting by the roadside or pushing a machine with either a dead engine or an empty petrol tank, no doubt wishing he had stayed at home and kept his few pounds in his pocket.

There's an old saying which says there's a fool born every minute, but as youth must be served and the wheels at least of progress kept revolving, motor cycle dealers sprang into business all over the country.

I remember one particular incident. A "Zenith Gradua" was bought for £30 and soon changed hands again at £60; this owner evidently not being too happy with his purchase. For when asked soon afterwards how he was getting on with it he replied: "Oh, I've sold it—found another fool!"

Money was by this time more plentiful. Thousands were being demobilised from the Armed Forces with gratuities based on length of service. Many of these men now back in civilian life were potential buyers and it was soon a case of the demand for motor cycles anyway to exceed the supply as production had not yet settled down to normal. It was not therefore unusual to have to pay a higher price for a used machine that it had cost when new. It seemed that the war had bridged the gap between horse-drawn and mechanical transport. Horses had been man's only means of transport from time immemorial.

It was only to be expected in these changed conditions that people would look to cars and motor cycles for sport and racing, one of the oldest of all sports, soon found many adherents.

One of the first racing circuits was the Brooklands basin-shaped track at Weybridge, Surrey, where the track was banked to give greater speed on the bends. Road racing being prohibited in this country, motor cyclists were obliged to look elsewhere for excitement, and so, as there were no such restrictions in the Isle of Man the "Tourist Trophy Races" were started there in 1907 and have continued to draw enormous crowds from all over the world for more than sixty years. The winner of the first Isle of Man "T.T." race was C. R. Collier on a 3½ h.p. "Matchless" at an average speed of 38.22 m.p.h.; the second being Rem Fowler on a 5 h.p. twin "Norton."

At that time there was no limit to engine capacity but a single cylinder machine was required to cover ninety miles and a "twin" at least seventy-five miles per gallon. In 1908 the petrol allowance was however reduced to one hundred and eighty miles respectively. In the year 1909 it became a race pure and simple for then the limit of miles per gallon was abandoned. For the record it was also in 1909 that pedalling gear was barred for the first time.

Since those days and owing to the tremendous support the races had it was found necessary to hold several races for different capacity engines from the ultra-lightweight of about 175 c.c. to 250 c.c., 350 c.c. and 500 c.c., the last mentioned being known as the "Senior" Race which was run on the last day of the series which was on a Friday. Owing to the great improvements in machines and engine design the lap speeds over the last few years have risen enormously the course now being lapped at over 100 m.p.h.

To visit the Isle of Man to watch the T.T. Races is something to be remembered for a lifetime. After looking over our humble touring models to make sure they would survive the ordeal a bunch of enthusiasts would meet at an arranged point and start off at about 5-30 a.m. facing a journey of nearly one hundred and sixty-five miles each way. Leaving here on a Thursday morning, all being well, we would reach Birkenhead in the afternoon. In the twenties there was no tunnel from Birkenhead to Liverpool so our machines would have to be parked there with overalls strapped to the carriers. We would then proceed on foot to the ferry which would take us over the Mersey to Liverpool Docks.

If things had gone well on the road we could sometimes catch an early enough boat to get to Douglas that evening, but if not we would have to spend the night on board. On arrival we would hire a taxi and have a trip round the course. To cross the Mersey and see the great Lever birds on top of the buildings at Port Sunlight through the mist leaves an everlasting impression on the memory.

One trip to the Isle of Man that I shall never forget was the year when we rode the whole distance in heavy rain and arrived at Liverpool without a dry thread of clothing between us. We trooped into the first hospitable-looking restaurant we came to and the management at once very kindly offered to dry out our wet garments while we revived ourselves with a meal and hot drinks, clad only in soaking raincoats. One member of the party had managed to keep a pair of pyjamas reasonably dry. Thus attired we sat until our clothes were dry and we were able to get the night boat for Douglas, still in high spirits in spite of the wetting.

The Ford Car and Others

WHILE it is very true to say that America has much to thank Wiltshire for in the persons of George Washington and William Penn, Wiltshire has much to thank America for. One thing that I would like to mention is the fact that it was an American, Henry Ford, who made possible the phrase "Motoring for the Million" to become an established fact. How many thousands of these pioneer cars of the twenties, affectionately known as "Tin Lizzies" came into this country, no one will ever know. Owing to the disastrous fire at the County Hall some thirty or forty years ago many records were destroyed which may possibly have given some idea of the actual number registered.

These cars, I believe the first mass produced ones to roll off assembly lines were, in their day very outstanding not only for their reliability but also for their price. Listed at about £115 or £120 complete there was a spontaneous demand for it. Spares could be obtained practically everywhere and the engine would run on lubricating oil at 2s. 6d. per gallon.

Though very simple to operate, they were very far removed from the cars of today with their automatic gears and single foot controllability. Even before the First World War they were coming into the country and were eventually manufactured here on a very large scale. I will give a brief description of them which I think would be interesting, having driven them many thousands of miles in the '20's and '30's.

The springing, or suspension as it is now termed, was by transverse cross springs over the front and rear axles, the chassis being clamped by two bolts front and rear to the centre of the multi-leaf spring, the whole width of the fixing being about six inches. There was no automatic or self starter. The engine had to be started by swinging the handle which required to be pushed against a light spring to keep it out of engagement when released from the hand.

There was no foot accelerator. Fixed to the steering column and within reach of the hand were two levers, the one on the left side being ignition control, advance or retard, the one on the right controlling engine speed, and woe betide the man who swung the starting handle with the ignition fully advanced. These engines being of something like twenty horsepower could backfire in a most vicious manner, not only these "Ford" cars but those of any make with handle start. The safest way was by pulling the handle up and not pushing it down, although the latter was often necessary, also to swing through several revolutions before the engine would respond and come to life.

The "Ford" was fitted with three foot pedals. The left operated the two forward gears and were spring mounted so that for engaging first or low gear the pedal was depressed. The gears being of the Epicyclic type caused a friction band to tighten and hold the gear. When changing up it was only necessary to release the pedal which automatically engaged the high or top gear.

The hand brake lever when pulled on would pull on mechanism acting on the gears and disengage the high gear pulling on the rear brakes at the same time. It was very dangerous to attempt to start the engine without first setting the handbrake or the vehicle would immediately run forward. The centre foot pedal operated the reverse gear, but before depressing it the hand brake had to be drawn to the vertical position to disengage the high gear.

The third pedal operated by the right foot was the foot brake and this also tightened a band in the gear box. There were no brakes on the front wheels.

During cold weather when the oil and gear band were liable to become sticky or tacky the usual procedure was to jack up one of the rear wheels so that it could all revolve together, the spinning of the jacked wheel helping to keep the engine turning.

Once the engine fired you had to get into your seat and operate the gear pedals until they were free and then pull the handbrake hard on, sometimes blocking the wheels, otherwise no sooner was the jack removed than the car would run forward with disastrous results.

In those days it was quite common for a man to get his arm broken or badly sprained when starting cars or lorries by a backfire, but the wise man when swinging the starting handle always kept his thumb in line with his fingers and did not grip the handle with his thumb. There was then a chance of the handle being torn from his hand without doing much injury.

Spare wheels as such hardly existed, the majority of cars having detachable rims which could be removed from the wheel with the tyre and the new replacement fitted usually by four bolts and clamps.

Motoring sometimes called for much ingenuity on the part of the driver. It was not unknown for a vehicle to have to be driven up a steep hill in reverse gear if the lowest forward gear was too high or with some makes of car where the petrol was gravity fed to the carburettor and the petrol tank at the rear. It was then only possible to surmount the hill by reversing the car so that the petrol tank was on a higher level than the carburettor.

Naturally the speed performance of some of these cars was not very high, which perhaps, was just as well. But for the popular "Ford Tourer" there was on the market a device known as the "Ford Super Gear" which could be fitted at the rear of the existing gear box. It meant fitting a shorter drive shaft. Fitted as an extra this gave quite a good turn of speed and could be used when the vehicle was running lightly loaded which was a great advantage.

I would hazard a guess that motoring in the twenties and early thirties was cheaper than at any time before or since. The "Morris 8" which could be bought for £100 and the "Austin 7" at a little more were both family cars. With the "Ford" at around £115, petrol about 1s. 3d. per gallon and the Road Fund Licence £1 per horsepower I can only finish this chapter by repeating the old familiar saying "Those were the days."

Swindon Tram Disaster

LOOKING through a copy of the *Swindon Evening Advertiser* for June 2nd, 1906 there was this headline: "Fatal Tram Accident." A tram had careered out of control down Victoria Hill while carrying visitors and local residents who had been attending the Bath and West Agricultural Cattle and Horse Show which was being held in Swindon that year. On the left hand bend opposite the Old Theatre it jumped the points and fell towards the right hand side of the street narrowly missing a horse and trap.

Unfortunately, as was to be expected, there were many casualties, three persons being killed and twenty-two reported injured whose names were given besides two others unidentified at the time of going to press, making twenty-four in all. One of the injured was Mr. Richard Townsend, a Miller and Corn Merchant from Chalford, near Stroud, who was well known in this locality. This tragedy might well have struck Minety as Mr. Richard Read, a local farmer, and Mr. A. M. Clarke, Baker and Corn Merchant of Silver Street, Minety, had both entered the tram at the top of the hill but as it was overloaded had decided to get off and walk, thus, quite probably, saving their lives.

CHAPTER FOUR

Minety's connections with America

The Penns

WILTSHIRE has many connections with the now great continent of America. The Washington family lived at one time in the north of the county and tablets or tombs to ancestors of George Washington are to be seen in Garsdon Church, near Malmesbury.

Within a couple of miles from there is "Penn's Lodge", which has associations with the Penn family, one of whom was the founder of Pennsylvania, and it has been claimed by some was born and buried at Minety, although there is no evidence to prove this. It has also been said and written that a tombstone, or parts of one, was laid in Minety St. Leonard's Church, that William Penn was buried before the Altar and that during repairs and alterations at the turn of the nineteenth/twentieth centuries the evidence of this was destroyed.

As recently as the nineteen-sixties an exhaustive survey was carried out by a direct descendant of William Penn—Brigadier O. F. G. Hogg, C.B.E., F.S.A., F.R.H.S., there being many missing links in the chain. As a result of his investigations he has written a book entitled *Further Light on the Ancestry of William Penn*, published by the Society of Genealogists, which shows that at least two of his ancestors were buried at Minety.

Brigadier Hogg served in the Great War from August 1914 with the first contingent of Anti-aircraft Artillery ever to accompany a British Expeditionary Force overseas. Then a subaltern, he took out No. 2 Section Anti-aircraft to France. There were six of these Anti-aircraft Sections all told, one for each of the six divisions of the B.E.F. The first two sections to proceed overseas (Nos. 1 and 2) sailed from Southampton in the *SS Palm Beach* on the 26th August 1914 and disembarked at Havre. No. 2 Section Anti-aircraft was posted to the 3rd Division of the 111 Corps. The guns were 1 pdr Q.F. (the S.A. pom-pom gun) mounted on high angled carriages.

As the last of the Penn family, George Penn, died in 1632, thirty years before the first entry in the Register at Minety Church, there is no mention of the Penns on record there. It is thought that the Penn's property could have been sold to the Pleydells in the latter part of the sixteenth century and that they then ceased to reside here.

The genealogical table of the Penns of the county of Wiltshire and the county of Gloucestershire which goes back to John Penn, d. *c.* 1560, does not mean that he was the first of the Penns to reside at Minety. They may well have been here for several generations. The following extract from *Wiltshire Notes and Queries* certainly helps to fill in some of the gaps:—

No. 76.   December 1911.   (Quarterly 1/6d.)

WILTSHIRE NOTES AND QUERIES.
Edited by Rev. F. H. Manley, M.A.
PENN OF RODBOURNE.

At Minety the only memorial that Aubrey could find of the Pennes was, he tells us, a broken gravestone near the south door of the Chancel, on which no more was visible than the letter "P," but which he knew marked the spot where lay William Penn, the ancestor of the founder of Pennsylvania.

66

Canon Jackson, some 200 years after, was able to decipher the inscription as "William –enn Dyed the 12 March in the . . . of Our Lord 1591." Unfortunately this stone seems now to have disappeared, probably in the course of some alterations made in the Chancel within the last twenty years.

As Minety registers previous to the restoration have vanished, we have no means of tracing the different members of the family who were buried or baptised in the Church.

Their Minety estate is said to have been sold soon after 1591 to the Pleydells. "Penn's Lodge" in the parish of Brinkworth mentioned by Aubrey still bears that name but he seems to imply that it was not identified with his Minety estate. It goes on:— In the transcripts of the registers at Salisbury is the following entry:

"1632. Mr. George Penne of ye parish of Brinkworth was buried at Minety 5th day of November."

Penns Lodge. Map ref. ST.026861.
Previous to 1932 this was occupied by Mr. Walter Keene. About this time it was purchased by Mr. Philip Slade and is now being farmed by Mrs. L. L. Slade and her two sons.

William Penn the celebrated founder of Pennsylvania was born in London on the 14th of October 1644. At the age of fifteen he was entered as a Gentleman Commoner at Christ Church, Oxford. He was a man of very strong religious beliefs and while there he suffered much for his outspoken views and eventually became a Quaker.

At that time the Quaker movement was going through a period of depression and three times he was apprehended and thrown into prison. The first time was in Ireland in 1667 and again in 1670. Soon after his release his father died and left him a clear estate of £1,500 a year which was a considerable amount in those days. He was, however, soon in trouble again and committed to Newgate for six months.

In 1672, on returning from Holland and Germany and being now twenty-eight years of age, he married Gulielma Maria, daughter of Sir William Springett, of Darling, in Sussex.

William Penn's first connection with America was in 1675 when he settled a dispute between two men who owned land in New England called New Jersey.

When Penn's father, Admiral Sir William Penn, died he was owed by the Government of Charles II £16,000 for moneys lent and arrears of pay. As his heir Penn was entitled to this, in lieu of the money he proposed that the Government should make him a grant of a tract of land in New England. On March 4th, 1681 a Royal Charter was granted to Penn constituting him full and absolute proprietor under the British crown of all the land he had petitioned for.

On September 1st, 1682 William Penn first set out for New England on the *Welcome*, a ship of three hundred tons burden, with about one hundred emigrants, mostly Quakers. During the voyage smallpox broke out and about thirty of them died. After six weeks at sea they anchored in the Delaware River.

Penn took up the cause of the Negroes and heartily condemned the slave trade. He made several journeys back to England trying to persuade the Government to improve their lot. It is said that any advance in the arts of civilised life in the early part of the eighteenth century by Indian tribes of the north west were due originally to William Penn.

He spent the last sixteen years of his life working entirely for others. With old age, failing health and financial problems to worry him, he eventually sold his rights to the Government for £12,000. This bargain was never completed. William Penn had now become very ill, suffering three apoplectic fits, and although he lingered on for some time, he died at Ruscombe in Berkshire on the 30th of July, 1718, in the seventy-fourth year of his age. He was buried in the Quaker burial ground at "Jordan's Meeting House," Beaconsfield, Bucks., where his tombstone may be seen.

Mr. Albert Waldron, a native of Minety, while serving in France as a driver with the Royal Army Service Corps in the 1939–45 War happened to pick up a piece of paper. On it he was surprised to see a picture of Minety Church together with an account of the life of William Penn. It was published on October 14th, 1944, exactly three hundred years after Penn's birth. This was a remarkable coincidence. Although damaged and rather worn the paper is all still readable, and understandably, a treasured item among Mr. Waldron's war souvenirs.

While on the subject of connections between Wiltshire and America it is fitting to record the fact that a family of tenant farmers from "The Moor Farm," Minety migrated to America in the year 1838. They evidently found it impossible to break the ties with the "Old Country." For in 1937 I received a postcard which, incidentally, the postmark bore the date of my fortieth birthday, August 8th, 1937, 11 a.m., Hicksville, Ohio. The postcard bears a picture of "The Moor Farm" from a pencil drawing on one side and is addressed to Mr. Leonard Manners, Minety, Wiltshire, England. It carries the following text:

> "Hicksville, Ohio,
> August 7th, 1937.
> This is a picture of 'Moor Farm House' near Minety, Wiltshire, England, tenanted by William Boulton and family at the time of their migration to Milan, Ohio in 1837. Yourself and family are earnestly invited to assist in the Centenary observance of this immigration by being present at the 29th annual reunion of his descendants at Lake Oliver, LeGrange County, Indiana, Thursday, August 19th.
> Yours sincerely,
> GEORGE D. SIMMONDS, Secretary."

TABLE IV

THE PENNS OF Co. WILTS AND Co. GLOUCESTER

John Penne of Minety d c 1560

William Penn of Minety. Buried before the altar in Minety Church. Died 12th March 1591/92. Will dated 1st May 1590. Proved 21st April 1592 (P.C.C.).

William Penn. Law clerk at Malmesbury. Chief clerk to Christopher George, counsellor-at-law. Died between 1587 and 1590 === Margaret, daughter of John Rastall, alderman of Gloucester and Ann George, sister of Christopher George

Ann Penn === Mr. Greene / Elizabeth Greene.

George Penn, Preservator, Keeper and Officer of Braydon Forest. b c 1570, buried at Minety 5.11.1632

Giles Penn, Captain R.N. b c 1573. Merchant of Bristol. Consul at Sallee === 5.11.1600 === Joan Gilbeart of Somerset

William Penn, Merchant at Bristol with his brother

Maria Penn | Sara Penn | Susanna Penn

Ensign William Penn, Clerk to the Cheque at Kinsale d 1676

George Penn b 1601 d.s.p. August 1664 === A Spanish Lady (divorced 1646)

Admiral Sir William Penn b April 1621, d 16.9.1670. Buried at St. Mary Redcliffe Bristol. Will dated 20.1.1669/70. Proved 6.10.1670 (P.C.C.) === 1643 === Margaret van der Schure (widow), daughter of Johann Jasper of Rotterdam. d 1682

Rachael Penn baptized 24.2.1607

Eleanor Penn d 24.11.1612

Gulielma, daughter and heir of Sir William Springett of Darling, Sussex. b February 1644 d 23.2.1694 (1st wife) Buried at Jordans === 4.2.1672 === William Penn, Founder of Pennsylvania b 14.10.1644 d 30.7.1718 Buried at Jordans === 5.3.1696 === Hannah, only daughter and heir of Thomas Callowhill of Bristol. b 18.4.1664 d 20.12.1726 (2nd wife) Buried at Jordans

Richard Penn d.s.p. April 1673

Margaret Penn d 1718 === 14.2.1667 === Anthony Lowther of Mask, Co. York d 1692

From "Further Light on the Ancestry of William Penn" by Brigadier O. F. G. Hogg, C.B.E., F.S.A., F.R.Hist.S., and published by The Society of Genealogists, 37, Harrington Gardens, London, S.W.7.

Unfortunately, we were not able to accept the invitation. I have since found out that one of the Boultons had, while living at Minety, married a Miss Westmacott and that about the time of the centenary function Miss Selena Ann Westmacott brought to the Moor Farm a Dr. Stopher from America. He was a doctor of music from Louisiana College of Music, a descendant of the Boulton family and was visiting England for the purpose of acquiring music from Novello's of London on behalf of the college. He said that he was determined to visit the old homestead while he was over here which he did. He asked me for a memento to take back and I found him an old wrought iron latch and drop ring off the old cowyard doors, rusty and old but he was more pleased than if I had given him a purse of gold.

As he shook hands with me on leaving he gave me a symbolic touch and asked "Do you know anything about that?" I said I did not and nothing more was said on the subject. I still have his Louisiana address but I have heard from a member of the Westmacott family that he has since died.

CHAPTER FIVE

Characters and cases

The Revd. T. A. Ludlow-Hewitt, M.A.

The Rev. T. A. Ludlow-Hewitt

A MAN TO BE REMEMBERED is the Reverend Thomas Arthur Ludlow-Hewitt, B.A., in charge of St. Leonard's Church, Minety, for over thirty years. Educated at Oriel College, Oxford, and a member of the Oxford Group, he was a very good living man, loved by his parishioners and played his part in parish affairs as much as could possibly be expected of him. As I was a member of the church choir and a member of the Board of School Managers I saw quite a lot of him, he being chairman and Correspondent. He was gifted with the art of being able to pass some witty remark whatever the matter under discussion. On one occasion at a school managers' meeting we were looking through testimonials of applicants for the post of Mistress for the Silver Street School. One or other of the members would remark from time to time as they read them, "Oh, this is a good one." It happened that there were seventeen applicants, so eventually the Vicar, who was also scrutinising them said, "You don't want to take any notice of those, you will find that they are all good."

We usually had a short gossip after the business of the meeting was over and he had declared the meeting closed. He was a master in the art of conducting a meeting. Sometimes he would say, "I'm sorry gentlemen, we cannot pass any resolution as we cannot form a quorum" and on a point of order he was there in a flash with "I'm sorry but you are out of order." In the event of a resolution being a tie when put to the meeting he could always determine the issue his way by casting his vote which was his privilege being chairman.

He used to tell a story of the offender who was hauled up before the magistrate for stealing. When asked if he had anything to say, "Well yer honour" said he, "We've all got to live." "Oh no" said the magistrate, "I don't see that at all!"

I remember once we were having over a bit of local gossip. Whether to believe it or not nobody seemed to know. The Vicar, as always, able to provide an answer said to us, "If you take my advice you'll believe half that you see and nothing that you hear."

Besides being a good sportsman he was also a very talented musician, able to play almost any stringed instrument and often taking his place at the Wiltshire Musical Festivals by playing in the orchestra. As our choirmaster he entered us in various classes for village choirs and small choral societies. We had to attend choir practices for periods of at least six months in preparation for these contests, taking the pieces one page at a time until he was completely satisfied, then the whole piece. Always before the event took place he would have Mr. Samuel Underwood (Uncle Sam to close friends) who was a professional teacher of singing to put us through our pieces and also conduct us at the festival. In this field our Vicar shewed his talents by the results he achieved, we on our part being also dedicated and enthused. There were very few contests we did not win at some time or other. We were also entered in Vocal Quartette classes in which we had our share of success.

In the year 1935 which was the Jubilee Year of King George V and Queen Mary we sang at the Cheltenham Musical Festival where we were also prize-winners.

This Festival preceded the "Royal Command" Concert at the Royal Albert Hall, London, and great was our surprise when we received a "Royal Command" to take part and to sing with the Royal Choral Society.

As the limitations of time and space were severe and the Royal Choral Society consisted of four hundred voices, the organisers were obliged to ask the secretaries of about two hundred prize-winning choirs to select four singers only.

Those honoured to represent Minety Church Choir were the Misses Annette and Dorinda Ludlow Hewitt, Mr. George Taylor and myself. The combined choirs numbered nearly seventeen hundred voices—gathered from all parts of England, Scotland, Wales and Ireland, the Channel Islands and the Isle of Man, each being given the opportunity of singing some of their own typical melodies. White tie and tails were the order of the day. Not being in possession of such raiment myself, I hastily took off on a visit to a friend who was about my height and build, as "needs must" when driven to it as the saying goes. He proved a friend indeed and I was able to leave for London carrying in a suitcase a perfectly good and well-fitting evening suit, when the great day arrived. We assembled at Silver Street; George Taylor driving us to Swindon, continuing the journey from there by train.

There was a full dress rehearsal during the afternoon and to assist us we were more or less intermingled with the Royal Choral Society. During the singing of one of the pieces, the conductor, not perfectly satisfied, stopped us all and asked us to mark a certain passage "Pianissimo." Without thinking too much I just pencilled a 'P,' not having noticed that sitting on my right was a member of the "Royal" who quietly said, "That's not Pianissimo. That's Piano'" Realising the standards of the company I was in I was very careful not to make any more such blunders if I could possibly help it.

The most famous Conductors of the day were taking part. The late Sir Henry Wood, the then Master of the King's Music, also the late Sir Malcolm Sargent, who had not then received his Knighthood. This I shall always look back on as the highlight of my career. If ever my life was spared so that I could achieve something great, this I feel must have been it. Whilst the Rev. T. A. Ludlow Hewitt was so talented, he was a very modest type of gentleman and never enjoyed the very best of health, once surviving a very severe illness.

World War I came along and his three sons immediately became involved. Alfred, then engaged in farming, was commissioned in the Army, served throughout the war, and at the end of hostilities was a Captain in the Army Service Corps. Soon however he was back to the call of the land, farming at Deerhurst, Gloucestershire where he established one of the best known and highest milk-yielding herds of Friesians in the country. He was often to be seen in the auction ring at Gloucester Market.

Edgar, who joined the Royal Irish Rifles, was not destined to remain for long in that branch of the Services. He had higher aspirations. It was very necessary that we should have fighters in the air as well as on land and sea. And so it was not long before he applied for a transfer to the Royal Flying Corps, as this branch was originally known. He thereafter made this his career and served with distinction throughout the war. By 1924 he had risen to the rank of Air Commodore. At the commencement of World War II he held the rank of Air Chief Marshal, became Chief of Bomber Command and was afterwards appointed A.D.C. to His Majesty King George VI, receiving a Knighthood in recognition of his service to his king and country.

The Vicar's third and youngest son, Cedric, was still at college at the outbreak of war. He, however, joined the Public Schools Corps and was afterwards commissioned in the Worcestershire Regiment with which he served in France, being severely wounded in 1917. From this, unfortunately, he never fully recovered.

Both of the Vicar's daughters gave their services as nurses so that all of the family were engaged in the war effort. This is something of which any family could be proud. The Vicar himself was, at the outbreak of war, far past the age of active service, although earlier in his life he had been Honorary Chaplain to the Third Wessex Brigade. A widower for a number of years, his daughters resided with him up to the time of his death in 1936, after which they both married. The eldest became Mrs. George Taylor (of Taylor's Printing Works) while the younger married Canon Sole who at that time held the living and resided at Crudwell.

Truth is indeed stranger than fiction for it does seem a coincidence that in the 1890's the Rev. John Edwards, M.A., was Vicar of Minety and one of his daughters also married a local young man by the name of Taylor.

T. M. Taylor

THIS Tom Taylor was a friend of my father's and about the same age. They both sang in the St. Leonard's Church Choir in the days when the organ and gallery were in the west end of the nave. He was apprenticed as a carpenter and wheelwright, etc. with Maurice Edmunds Miles of Askew Bridge. After a serious illness he was recommended to take a sea voyage. This apparently did him much good as he came back and married Miss Edwards, afterwards I believe moving to London. When my parents were married in 1895 he gave them a very nice china cabinet with glass doors which he himself had made, and which is still in use in my home and in very good condition.

The sea voyage he took for his health was to South Africa on a sailing ship. The return voyage took altogether six months as the following letter he wrote to my father will show:—

Cape Town,
South Africa
February 28th, 1886

Dear Henry,

I think I promised you a letter when I saw you last but I have not time to write much. I arrived here quite safe on Tuesday, the 16th of February. The weather was very favourable all the voyage. I found it very cold in the Channel. After being out a week we found it get warmer every day. Christmas Day the sun was shining quite strong. We were in the North Atlantic then, but could not help wishing I was at Minety sitting by the fire and taking part in some amusing game. Our cook spoilt the plum pudding by mixing a lot of salty fat with it. I will leave you to guess what it tasted like.

Our usual diet is salt beef and soup on Tuesdays, Thursdays and Saturdays. On Sundays we have preserved **fresh** meat and soup. For breakfast and tea we have **hard** biscuit and butter. Our drink is coffee and tea. It was a long time before I could make a meal off any of it but I was bound to eat that or nothing. How would you like to be tied to it for two months?

I live in what they call the Aft Deck with the carpenter, cooks and two apprentices. The sleeping places are like cupboards in a wall six feet long by two feet wide. Sometimes I nearly tumble out when the vessel is rolling. You would laugh to see how careful we have to be at mealtimes to prevent the food from upsetting.

As we neared the line I found it getting very hot. I had to leave my coat and waistcoat off. We crossed the line on January 11th. We had several heavy squalls that day. On the following Saturday we were becalmed and we did not get any wind for four days. I was working with the carpenter and the heat was almost unbearable.

We sighted land on Monday, February 15th, about 11 a.m., but a headwind sprung up and we could not get into the Bay until Tuesday. We laid at anchor in Table Bay all day Tuesday. On Wednesday we were towed into the dock. I was soon on shore having a look round. Cape Town is built at the foot of Table Mountain, so called because it is flat on the top.

All the principal works belong to the Government and the work is done by convicts divided into small gangs with an armed soldier to guard them. Fruit is very cheap, especially grapes. I can get a large basket for 9d. Cattle are cheap too. You can buy a very good horse for £2, but they are not as large as English horses. Nearly all the cows are black, something like the Irish cattle. Milk is 3d. a pint and fresh butter 1s. 6d. a pound in the summer. I am told it used to be 3d. a pound. It is nearly all Dutchmen that keep the farms.

There are lots of Malays, Kaffirs and Hottentots about here. The Malays are the most civilised. They are very fond of fine dresses, especially the women. There are a great many English here too. All the English people born here are called "Africandas." I have been to the Cathedral twice which is a very fine building but of modern style. It was a treat to be able to join in the service after going nine Sundays without.

We have finished discharging our cargo (which was done chiefly by niggers). Tomorrow, Monday, we start for Nolloth to take in our homeward bound cargo. No wonder we couldn't find that place on the map. It has only been used as a port since they found the copper ore mines which, I am told, was about five years ago. I will finish this letter when we get to Port Nolloth, then I shall be able to tell you a little about it.

MARCH 25TH. We left Cape Town on Monday, March 1st and arrived here in Port Nolloth on the 4th. It is not at all a nice place to come to owing to there not being a dock. So we have to lay at anchor about a mile from the shore. It is a very rough place. When the wind is calm there is a very heavy swell on the sea. A vessel called the "Veronica" was lying here about a fortnight before we arrived at the Cape. She had just finished taking in her cargo when it came on to blow a very heavy breeze, causing her to break her anchor chain, and before they could let go the other anchor she had drifted into another vessel called the "Marquis of Worcester" and in less than an hour went down. The crew just managed to save themselves by getting into some more ships. They were put on shore and sent to Cape Town and from there they have come to England in the Mail Steamer. We are lying close to where she went down. There is no chance of getting foul of her as we have 900 feet of cable out, which shows the water must be very deep.

No one is allowed on shore as the sea is too rough for a boat. The copper ore is brought out in small vessels called "lighters." The Company keeps a small steamer to tow them out and the Captains go ashore with that. Our Captain has promised to take me on shore before we leave. All we can see from here is a lot of huts (occupied by Hottentots) and a high range of mountains at the back.

The copper ore mines are several hundred miles up the country. They have a line of rails from the mines down to here but they cannot use an engine on them owing to the quantity of sand there is here, which will not allow the metals to lie firm enough. So they use mules to draw the trucks and it takes them a week to go and come back.

Our cargo will be all in next week when we shall leave for Swansea and expect to be home by the end of June. I am much better for my trip, but I hope to improve more on the passage home.

74

You will hardly know me as I have allowed my whiskers to grow. Please tender my respects to your mother and father, etc., and also to any enquiring friends, hoping this will find you all well.

No doubt you are obliged to wear overcoats now, but I have it quite warm. You may let Herbert read this if you like. I would have written to him but have not much time.

I remain,

Yours very sincerely,

T. M. Taylor

E. E. Taylor

ONE Wiltshire man whose name will be a household word for many generations was Ernest Edward Taylor.

Born in Minety in 1869, he was a self educated man, ambitious from boyhood. He had the gift of looking ahead and evidently decided that printing was an industry with a future.

It was in 1884, nearly one hundred years ago, that he obtained an old hand press and commenced a one man printing business. In the meantime he had realised the necessity of being able to write shorthand as an aid to his many and varied means of earning a livelihood. Reporting news for the Press was one of the most important of his activities. Building a house at the commercial end of Minety, Silver Street, with his first Printing Works built nearby, he opened a shop adjoining which was run by his wife. Here Mrs. Taylor sold cards, writing materials, fancy goods, patent medicines, sweets, tobacco and cigarettes, etc.

E. E. Taylor, the man. Founder of the Printing Works.

Ernest Taylor was without a doubt the first man in Minety to advertise for sale "Motor Spirit and Ammunition," this in the first decade of the century at a time when with the biggest stretch of the imagination there were not more than two motor cars and one motor cycle in the village, the motor cycle being owned by Frederick Hinder who kept the Silver Street Post Office. I feel quite safe in making this statement although I was very young at the time, as things mechanical had a particular fascination for me and left an indelible impression on my mind.

He was a great "after dinner speaker" with a wonderful vocabulary and flow of language, was never at a loss for words and could praise or humiliate to suit his prevailing mood or need. He also possessed a good Bass voice and sang in the Church Choir for many years. As a young man he was proficient on a wind instrument being a member of the Church Orchestra, with a particular liking for the trombone. I shall never forget our Harvest Festivals when year after year the St. Leonard's Church was filled to capacity at the Evening Service, some to give thanks, some to listen to the music and the choir and some to listen to the Sermon. The Hymn that Ernest Taylor most enjoyed singing was No. 383: "We plough the fields and scatter," and when we came to the refrain: "All good gifts around us" Taylor could not resist the impulse to come in with a vocal impromptu which resembled a flourish on the trombone: "All good gifts DA DA DA are sent from Heaven above" sung with a twinkle in his eye that I shall never forget.

As many as possible of his family of ten were brought into the business which prospered and flourished on the original site. The works have been extensively enlarged and modern machinery installed and today the firm of Taylor and Sons under George and Raymond, his sons, are the largest employers of labour in the parish with at least two dozen men and women to handle the huge amount of work that pours in, a fine example of enterprise, advertisement and service.

A great sportsman, a good shot and a great follower of the Turf; if "E. E. Taylor" could not give you a tip of the 2.30 you may depend on it 'twas no good asking anyone else.

There was nothing he enjoyed better for relaxation than a pint at the "Red Lion" and a game of dominoes or "Halfpenny Nap." One Christmas in the '20's our Church Organist, Mr. Glazebrook, had invited the members of the Choir to a party at his home at Edge, near Stroud. Snow was falling as we left Minety to cross the Cotswolds. The solid tyred coach was making fair headway until we had passed through Stroud and were starting to climb Pitchcombe Hill which was almost at the end of the journey. The snow had continued to fall heavily and was by this time almost a foot deep on the road. All the men got out and tried to push but with no grip whatsoever the wheels were spinning unmercifully. Eventually we all had to abandon the coach and walk the rest of the way. We had a wonderful party and towards midnight it was obvious that we could not possibly return home by road that night but would have to wait until morning and take the train from Stroud G.W.R. By this time supplies of liquid refreshment were naturally running low and the seriousness of the situation for some was becoming desperate, our host being a tee-totaller. Nothing daunted, Taylor sallied forth in the snow in coat and muffler to the nearest public house. It was well past closing time and the irate landlord roused from his sleep refused to serve him, whereupon Taylor told him in no uncertain manner that as we were genuine travellers stranded for the night he was obliged by law to do so and even to put us up for the night if requested to. This he further stressed by telling the unfortunate landlord that if he refused his request he would attend the next Licencing Session and raise an objection to the renewal of his licence.

Needless to say the beer was immediately forthcoming and on his return we were able to sit down and prepare for a game of "Nap" to while away the time till morning.

Mrs. Glazebrook took charge of the ladies who disappeared as if by magic while cards were soon found for the men. We played "Halfpenny Nap" until

6 a.m. when after cups of tea and light refreshments we all walked down to Stroud. There were still six "doubles" to be played off and I had won just sufficient to pay my train fare from Stroud to Minety Station.

One of Taylors' most successful enterprises was the publication in 1890 of *Taylor's Directory* with a caption on the cover stating that it covered:

"Malmesbury, Cirencester and District, Purton, Wootton Bassett, Cricklade and all surrounding villages.
Ready Reckoner, Market and Livestock Tables, Legal Notes, Illustrated Almanac, Cash Diary and complete local Telephone Directory."

This publication was a best seller. Having names and addresses of everyone in the districts covered and so much valuable information in its pages as time went on it became quite indispensable. In fact, this book became so popular that after fifty years of its introduction it was in greater demand than ever. It was also a good advertising medium made much use of by local professional and tradesmen.

Taylor's original "Express" Printing Works consisted of a large one-roomed building with a hand press at one end and surrounded by racks and shelves of type, large and small. His office was a small room in the dwelling house. This gradually filled with documents, dockets, etc. As the business expanded, so too did the family. This office fast becoming inadequate and the room being required for domestic purposes he found it necessary to put up a separate building for the purpose. Just at that time some friends of mine by the name of Whitting of "Old Park" Farm, Charlton, were retiring from farming and Mr. Taylor was able to buy a large sectional building that had been used as a workshop by them. In a photograph of myself taken with my first motor-cycle—a four cylinder 5 h.p. F.N.—at "Old Park" in 1916, this building can be seen in the background. Needless to say the sight of this building which has been standing at the Printing Works for so many years brings back happy memories to me of the days when young Robert Whitting and myself had spent so many hours together in the workshop learning the mysteries of the Internal Combustion Engine.

During my many years association with Ernest Taylor I was frequently visiting him during office hours. Always before taking leave of him a bottle of beer would be produced as if "from the hat" which was shared between us with perhaps an appropriate tale to close the interview. (Here Here!)

Never at a loss for a song he was always ready with one at the Annual Choir Supper at the Vicarage. I well remember a particular favourite of his which never failed to hold the audience and which had a rousing chorus that everyone joined in. It ran something like this:

"What a fine hunting day, 'tis as balmy as May
And the hounds to the village will come.
Every friend will be there and all trouble and care
Will be left far behind them at home.
See servants and steeds on their way
And sportsmen their scarlet display
Let us join the glad throng that goes laughing along,
And we'll all go ahunting today."

Chorus:
We'll all go ahunting today,
All nature looks smiling and gay,
So we'll join the glad throng
That goes laughing along
And we'll all go ahunting today.

Farmer Hodge to his dame says I'm sixty and lame
    Times are hard yet my rent I must pay.
But I don't care a jot if I raise it or not,
    For I will go ahunting today
There's a fox in the spinney they say,
    We shall find him and get him away,
I'll be first in the rush and ride hard for the brush
    So I must go ahunting today.
Chorus.

There's a doctor in boots, with a diet that suits him
    Of strong home brewed ale and good beef.
And his patients in pain say we've come once again
    To consult you in hope of relief.
To the poor, he advice gave away
    For the rich he prescribed and took pay,
But to each one he said "You will shortly be dead
    If you don't go ahunting today."
Chorus.

As the Judge sits in court he gets wind of the sport
    For the lawyers apply to adjourn
As no witnesses come and there's none found at home
    They have followed the hounds and the horn.
Says His Worship "Great fines they must pay
    If they will not our summons obey,
Yet it's very fine sport, so we'll break up the court
    And we'll all go ahunting today."
Chorus:
    We'll all go ahunting today,
        All nature looks smiling and gay,
    So we'll join the glad throng
        That goes laughing along,
    And we'll all go ahunting today.

Miles' and Ancestors

I THINK it safe to say that among many other names long associated with Wiltshire, such as Waldron, Maskelyn, Cole, Packer, Smart, Clarke, Jones, Knapp, Hiscock, Hinder, Brown, Westmacott and Timbrell, the name of Miles will linger as long as any. We still have a silver teapot which was presented to a Miles in 1857, the inscription reading as follows:

    "Presented to Maurice Edmunds Miles for 30 years Faithful Service as Parish Clerk of Minety. Easter 1857."

The testimonial which accompanied it reads:

    The Testimonial presented to Maurice Edmunds Miles after 30 years Faithful Service as Parish Clerk of Minety was subscribed for by the following persons.

        Rev. Canon Tuson. Vicar.
        Captain Perry Keene.
        Miss Luxmoore.
        Mrs. Boulton.
        Mr. Cole.
        Mr. Jonathan Packer.
        Mr. Henry Hiscock.
        Rev. William Maskelyn. Once Curate of Minety.

Captain Maskelyn. 20th Regiment.
Miss Bettison.
Mr. Perratt.
Mrs. Wallis.
Mr. Hall.
Mr. Vizar.
Mrs. Ann Hiscock.
Mrs. Moreton.
Mr. William Ellison.
Thomas Peacy Keene Esq.
Abraham Hinder.
Mrs. Manners.
Mrs. George Vizar.
Mrs. Knapp.
Mr. Westmacott.
Mr. Greenslade.
Mrs. Keene.
Mrs. Pearce Brown.
Miss and Master Edward Tuson.
Thomas Clark.
James Smart.
Thomas Edwards.
Mr. William Peacey.

On Easter Tuesday evening 1857 the subscribers drank tea together at the National Schoolroom when Maurice Edmunds Miles and his family were invited to meet them—and the Testimonial was presented.

FREDK. E. TUSON, *Vicar.*

The Miles family have for generations carried on the trade or craft of Carpenter, Wheelwright, Sawyer, Builder, etc. One Jesse Miles and another William Havilah being also organists at the Church. Havilah William, another Miles born in Minety in 1869 was also a wheelwright, builder and decorator, etc. in the village and was sexton at the church for over forty years.

There are many visible reminders of his work standing in Minety, at least ten houses including Silver Street House, where he lived for most of his married life. He it was who carried out the work of the underpinning of the church tower and the alterations to the interior of the church already mentioned.

In the late twenties he gave a piece of land centrally situated for the erection of a Village Hall. Until then the only places suitable for entertainments were the two schools, one at each end of the village. The hall was officially opened in 1930 by the late Mrs. Cecil Gouldsmith then of Minety House, and although it was a wooden structure it lasted until 1968 when again through the generosity of many local people (here should be mentioned the names of Major and Mrs. Crocker, the present owners of Minety House, and Mrs. Jonas) it was possible to erect a new hall of more permanent structure.

Although close on fifty years of age Havilah Miles was not to be left behind and before 1920 he learned to drive a car continuing to do so until he was nearly eighty years of age.

Joneses—Masons, etc.

A WORD should be said of the Jones family as for over a hundred years they were building in Cotswold stone in this district. Coming originally from Coate, Gloucestershire, they were craftsmen in this type of building. They were responsible for the building of St. Leonard's School in 1856 and the Silver Street School in

Havilah William Miles.
Carpenter, Builder, Wheelwright, Undertaker, Sexton and Chorister.

1875, besides, together with the firm of Miles, carpenters, wheelwrights and builders here for a similar number of years, practically all of the older houses in this parish. It was they who carried out the underpinning of the St. Leonard's Church in 1906–7 and also built the Bakery and bread ovens in Silver Street where the bread for the local inhabitants was baked for more than half a century.

As the changeover from stone to brick came they carried on as bricklayers and it is estimated that there are at least fifteen houses still standing in Silver Street and the Station Road alone that were built by them. The coming of the railway was the chief cause of more building being done in this area. Mr. Tom Jones and his sister Kate are the last of this family to reside in Minety, many of the younger generation having been attracted by the call to the towns.

The Joneses were staunch Primitive Methodists and for many years before the 1914–18 War took a great interest in the local Brass Band. With the help of voluntary labour they built the "Band Hall" in Silver Street, where they held their practices. A number of the male members of the family served in the war, some never to return and the Brass Band eventually had to disband and the Hall came into disuse. The survivors of the family handed it over to the Wiltshire County Council to be used for the benefit of the youth of the village and for several years it was used as an Infant School.

The house still occupied by Mr. and Miss Jones in Silver Street was copyhold until 1926 when the freehold was purchased by Mr. John Jones and the copyhold extinguished by payment to the then Lady of the Manor, Georgiana Poppoea Mullings. Many of the Minety properties were Copyhold until recent years and were liable to the Lord of the Manor for a nominal rent, a Relief of perhaps a few pence per year and a "Heriot" "when it should so occur." A "Heriot" is a kind of fine to be paid to the Lord of the Manor on the decease of a person holding land of the Manor and could consist of money or the best beast, jewel or chattel that belonged to the deceased. I am not sure if this custom still survives. It is possible that there are some properties that are still Copyhold and this can usually be ascertained by a careful scrutiny of the Title Deeds.

Joneses and Ted Walker

OLD JONES, the great grandfather of the present generation, who lived in Minety in the middle of the last century brought up a family of fourteen children. Most of them being boys followed the trade or calling of the family and likewise becoming stone masons and builders.

Neighbours, as always being curious besides liking to appear interested in the welfare of their acquaintances were of course anxious to know what the last arrival was, whether it was a son or a daughter. Well, it was another son to the great delight of his father who always looked on boys as potential breadwinners. It wasn't long before the question was asked, "Well, what is it this time?" to which the beaming father replied, "Oh, as usual, another gert mortar mixer."

Old Ted Walker who died in 1968 aged eighty-six had lived in Minety for the whole of his life farming as a small holder and doing all kinds of general work such as carpentry and building, a considerable amount of this with the Joneses. He told me that when the classroom at Silver Street school was added he helped the builders. So as to have a supply of water close at hand for mixing the mortar they dug a deep hole in the ditch on the opposite side of the road by what was then the "Allotment." He declared there was a spring close by because although the work was done in the summer and there was no rain there was always plenty of water in the hole for their requirements. This could well be true. He also said that where the Village Hall now stands on Hornbury Hill there is another spring as when this field was an "allotment" (which I can remember) he could never plough that part of the field as it was always wet and swampy. Old red drainpipes are often to be found by builders and others when digging out footings and foundations, lying three or four feet below the surface evidently the remains of a former drainage system.

In the heyday of the Great Western Railway Works at Swindon there was always, during the summer months, a great exodus of workers to the surrounding villages. These Railway employees were allowed a special privilege of cheap travel on the trains. I believe the return fare from Swindon to Minety was about four-pence. So every Saturday afternoon large numbers of them would get off at Minety Station and sally forth, north, south, east and west. Not only could they enjoy a breath of clean country air but they could also buy from the local farmers all kinds of fruit, apples, pears, etc., and pick blackberries when in season. They also bought rabbits when available. Besides baskets they also carried bags of the army kit-bag type which would hold nearly a bushel of apples.

We looked forward to these Saturday afternoons in those days with the expectancy of taking a bit of cash. Most of them would buy about two pecks (fourteen pounds in weight approximately) at a shilling a peck. This was less than a penny per pound. They first had one peck tipped into the bag, then tied the middle with string. Another peck would go into the top of the bag which was again tied. This made a load which was easy to carry over the shoulder leaving the hands free to carry other goods.

Old Ted Walker once told me of a time he had promised to get a rabbit for a would-be customer by the following Saturday. But by Friday night he had met with no success. Knowing where the rabbits came out of a burrow he waited till dusk and quietly walked within gunshot range of the hedge knowing that if he kept perfectly still one or two would soon make an appearance. He had been standing there silently and without moving for some considerable minutes when suddenly something hit him on the head and grabbed his hat. This made him jump and to his astonishment he found that, no doubt in the twilight, taking him for a post or a tree trunk a large brown owl had landed on his head. However, undaunted by this experience he waited there until he eventually got his rabbit, his chief concern being to keep his promise and not to disappoint his customer. Neither did he!

The Rustic Stile. This illustrates a "Footpath and Bridle Track" which may be used for the passage of horses either mounted or on the rein but not for wheeled vehicles. The rails, or "slip rails" are made to slide back to admit passage of the horse. The Rustic Stile and slip rail was used in many instances, being much cheaper to erect than a swing gate.
The recognised widths were three feet for a footpath, five feet for a bridle track and ten feet for a carriageway.

Lewis Slade

THE old Wiltshire family of Slade have farmed in this area for very many years. Lewis Slade was born at Lea and was married on November 5th, 1876. On November 6th he moved his goods and chattels to Minety by horse and wagon and is believed to be the last man to pay toll at the Minety Turnpike known as "Seven Bridges Gate." He paid toll on the first load but when he came to the gate with his second the tolls had been removed and he was allowed free passage. He lived near the railway station and besides farming he also carried on the business of coal merchant. For many years he was to be seen walking through the village with his horse and cart and a load of coal. A very staunch Conservative and Tariff Reformer and regular Church-goer he would not even read a Sunday newspaper. For many years he sang Tenor in the St. Leonard's Church choir and although he was slightly built he was an enthusiastic bell ringer, ringing the heaviest bell in the peal. A great walker, he regularly walked the two miles each way to and from Church, often twice on a Sunday and often have I accompanied him as far as the point where our ways parted. In those days everyone used the footpaths and to save mileage he could go

82

the whole distance by crossing the road in only one or two places. He told me once that the biggest fright of his life was when he was walking to Church one very dark night and stumbled into a horse which was lying close to the footpath. The horse jumped up taking him off his feet and throwing him to the ground.

Lewis Slade.
The last man to pay toll at Minety Turnpike, November 6th, 1876 (?)

At our annual Choir Suppers each member was expected to make some contribution to the entertainment, either by singing a song, reciting a poem or telling a story. When it came to Slade's turn his favourite song was one which sang the praises of "Tariff Reform" set to the tune of "Red, White and Blue." The chorus finished with "It's Bonar Law and Chamberlain for ever. Old England and Tariff Reform."

It was almost traditional for a farmer to keep a horse as long as it was able to work satisfactorily and remained sound on its four legs. Slade was no exception. His horse did the farm work such as manure carting and "bushing", which was going over the fields after the manure had been spread with a horse drawn wooden frame about eight feet wide interlaced with tough blackthorn bushes, which did the work now done by chain harrows of breaking down the manure, molehills, etc. to level and fine it down. However, as the story goes, Slade was on his round of the village delivering coal one day when without having shewn any sign of sickness his horse still harnessed to the cart fell suddenly to the ground. It was soon apparent to those who gathered around that the horse was dead. A sad blow indeed to Slade who remarked sadly, "He's been a good 'hoss' and in all the years I've had 'en its the first time he ever served I that trick."

Jack Freeth

A WELL KNOWN character in these parts in the latter part of the last century and the early part of the present one was Jack Freeth, referred to as "One-armed Jack". In his younger days he had been a groom. Like so many more of that generation when

John Freeth, otherwise known as "One Armed Jack."

intoxicants were cheap and public houses open all day, drink was eventually his downfall. The story is that he lost his arm when pulling a pig out of a cart by the tail. The pig's tail came off and old Jack fell causing the injury which cost him his arm, a lesson which, unfortunately for himself and the pig he learned too late.

In later years he earned a few odd shillings "cattle droving." He had no home and for many years slept in an old shed by the roadside just beyond Minety Station and sometimes in a cowshed by the railway line. In those days before road transport took over, cattle came by rail to Minety Station where there was a cattle pen and these "drovers" would hang around and drive them on foot (on the hoof it was called) to their final destinations.

On one Wootton Bassett market day George Read bought a bunch of cattle and gave old Jack the job of driving them to Minety. Before leaving him George gave him a shilling.

It was not far from the market place to Coped Hall and the "Prince of Wales" where Jack was soon settled in and the cattle left wandering on the roadside. It was the following morning before Jack eventually arrived at Minety and to make matters worse he had lost one animal which was not found until several weeks later.

Old Jack always carried a stout stick with a heavy knob handle and he knew how to use it. Even when eating or drinking this stick was tucked under his arm. I remember once seeing him with two or three companions come out of the "Old Red Lion" at Minety Station. Voices were being raised and Jack looked like being set upon by one of the others. Quick as a flash he gripped the knob of his stick in his teeth, slid his hand down, grasped it at the bottom and swung it over on to the other man's head and laid him out as flat as a pancake. He was a tough old customer and could be pretty dangerous when roused. Alas he eventually finished up in Malmesbury workhouse.

Tom Jefferies

TOM JEFFERIES was a very familiar sight at Swindon Market until the early thirties. Remembered by many and familiarly known as "Old No-arms," always wearing a bowler hat pressed well down on the back of his head, rather pale and sallow faced and always wearing a long overcoat. Helping with the cattle, waving his armless sleeves about, no Swindon Market would have been complete without him, and he was usually hired at the close by one of the buyers to take a bunch of cattle back to a farm. Having no arms was no drawback to him as the cattle seemed to take more notice of his flapping sleeves than they did of a stick. He was one of the last of the old cattle "Drovers" who always frequented the markets before mechanical transport took over.

Having investigated the matter as thoroughly as possible I feel safe in saying that Tom Jefferies lost his arms in an accident in the Swindon Great Western Railway Works and that he lived in a cottage in Telford Road, Moredon, Swindon, now known as Cheyney Manor Road. While in *Kelly's Directory* for 1903 a Thomas Jefferies is listed as living in Swindon.

I think a man such as this is worth putting on record as an example of courage in adversity. No doubt he could have been admitted to a "Workhouse" but he evidently preferred to earn his living and enjoy his freedom. On a market day in fine weather he was often to be seen outside a public house where a hunk of bread and cheese and a pint mug of beer had been placed on a back window ledge. He preferred to be left alone to eat this meal in his own way and drinking by taking the mug between his teeth. It is said that the farmers offered to subscribe to get him some artificial arms but that he refused to wear them. He would often walk ten or fifteen miles to attend a farm sale where he would invariably find employment. The money he earned was put into his outside pocket, No doubt when driving cattle long distances he spent the nights in barns and cowsheds.

I have just sketched him as I remember him.

Tom Jefferies, known as "Old No Arms."

George Cutts—Blind Basket Maker

GEORGE CUTTS who lived at Fritterswell, Brinkworth, was another character to be remembered. He is reported as having died there in October 1949. Although totally blind for fifty years he continued to earn his living by making a variety of baskets and rabbit nets. These he used to carry for many miles, to Purton, Cricklade, Minety, probably to Malmesbury and Wootton Bassett and even as far as Calne. It is said that it was impossible to deceive him with money as he knew every coin by feel. He also had an uncanny sense of hearing. He was often to be seen in public houses with his wares taking and delivering orders. In spite of his affliction he was always cheerful and smiling. Besides being adept at basket making he was also a good entertainer, singing to his own accompaniment on an old banjo, which he often brought with him. The song I best remember is that old favourite "The vly be on the Turmot." In my search for all the information I could get I approached Dr. B. L. Hodge of Malmesbury who told me that this song was the regimental song of the Wiltshire Regiment and that at each annual Reunion Dinner it was traditional, during the evening, for an officer to stand on a chair, one foot on the table and give a rendering of this song. He too remembered George Cutts, the blind basket maker who had made a square basket for use when his first baby daughter was born.

We ourselves have a basket made by him some thirty years ago and no doubt there are others still in use.

In the early twenties an auctioneer by the name of Charles Gale commenced holding a cattle market in the paddock behind the Vale Hotel at Minety. Besides all sorts of livestock, farm implements, large quantities of surplus war materials such as half hundredweight drums of paint, much useful timber from dismantled army huts and all kinds of carpenters' tools were auctioned. There you would regularly see old George Cutts with his baskets and a quantity of rabbit nets over his arm. As this district was at that time over-run with rabbits he could depend on finding a ready sale. It made no difference to him whether he made his journeys by day or by night and I have seen him leave the "New Red Lion" after ten-thirty at night tapping the road and grass verge with his stick.

Coming to Minety from Brinkworth he passed over Somerford Common and Ravensroost Farm, then occupied by Mr. Frank Hiett. There were several Poplar trees standing close to the road which Mr. Hiett had cut down. The next time George Cutts came along, he stopped to pass the time of day and in the course of conversation he said to Hiett, "I'm sorry you had those trees down. I miss them." "How do you mean?" said Hiett. "You couldn't see them." "No," replied Cutts, "But when I heard the wind rustling through those trees I knew where I was."

He used to keep pigeons and when he let them out he was able to follow their flight by sound and as they circled round he knew exactly where they were.

Post and Rails.

This stile is a typically North Wilts type where timber is in good supply while stone has to be brought a considerable distance. This particular one stood opposite the Silver Street School giving access to a footpath to the "Allotment" and beyond to the Lower Moor until a few years ago. Also shewn is the "Pollard Oak" standing in "Hinder's Field" (now farmed by Mr. Ron Read).

All disputes which arose during school hours were settled under this tree, the supporters of both parties forming a ring, the contestants stripping off their jackets and setting into each other—no rules—the fight only ending when one side had given in. Alas, I fear much blood was shed there in my day to which I seem to remember I contributed my full share.

The White Horse Hotel and the Hughes Family

THE WHITE HORSE HOTEL stands on the Minety and Ashton Keynes railway bridge, situated on the south side of the Malmesbury to Cricklade road, facing north and dominating the whole village. From there a wide expanse of the Cotswolds is visible to the north and the Marlborough Downs to the south. The indications are that there has been a building of some description on the site for many years, as the old vaults underneath the present building seem to extend almost under the road. In the old days it had stabling and accommodation for several horse-drawn conveyances which were hired by people getting off the train at the railway station "Minety and Ashton Keynes." This station served a wide area.

The hotel is a large three-storey building and for many years consisted of several tenements, the publican occupying the first floor which is on a level with the rising road. The lower floor was occupied by local labouring families. There was a balcony leading in from the road on the east side above the basement and leading round to some rooms at the back, also let as tenements. The bedrooms for these upper occupants were on the third floor. When I was very young an aunt of mine (Ann Vizer) lived there and I loved to walk round the balcony and gaze around. This balcony has now been taken down and the lower rooms used as cellars, the whole place now being run on the lines of a hotel. Before World War I the licence was held by Thomas Ratcliffe who married Kate Ponting, both local families. With high hopes of doing good business picking up passengers from the trains, Thomas became dissatisfied with his mode of transport and decided to change it for a car. The Model 'T' Ford was then being imported at a price of £120 new while on the second-hand market they were very cheap. And so the second-hand Ford was garaged in the old trap house facing the road on the brow of the hill so that directly the car left the garage it was necessary to brake to prevent it from running down the slope. Facing were the palings which divided the road from the station embankment with a gradient of one in two. Now Thomas was more accustomed to driving a horse than a car and cautiously took the seat behind the steering wheel whilst someone else cranked up the engine for him. Immediately the engine came to life the car headed straight for the palings. Thomas was taken completely by surprise and started pulling at the steering wheel and shouting "Whoa! Whoa! You b*****." but mechanical gears heeded not his frantic shouts and over the road and through the palings went the old Ford, Thomas as well. This so damped his enthusiasm that he was never seen driving on the road afterwards and it was a considerable time I remember before the palings were repaired.

In the ground floor of the "Vale" lived a large family by the name of Hughes. The six sons were named Abraham, Nathan, Eli, Eder, Ted and Fred. There were two daughters, one of them marrying Henry Freeth of Minety. They were good workmen, counting not their hours, spending most of their hard-earned wages in the public bar above which they reached by climbing the bank, through the railings which brought them to the level of the entrance.

One very big advantage they enjoyed was that however drunk they were, it only needed someone to give them a push through or over the railings and they would roll down the bank, coming to rest at their own front door.

Trustworthy, hardworking men as they were, probably from the old pioneer railway navvy stock and living within a few yards of a public house with five or six others within walking distance, they seldom went anywhere else. Being so accustomed to hard drinking it never affected them during working hours. They were never long without employment, navvying, building work or digging the flint at Flistridge which was used for roadmaking. The flint was loosened with pick-axes, thrown through a screen with shovels and hauled away with horses and tip-carts to be deposited in heaps by the roadside where it was to be used. It was then spread over the road, watered with watercarts drawn by horses and rolled in with the Council streamroller. Wages for flint digging were high in comparison to other such work. An ordinary worker earned about 12/- per week at the commencement of this century.

The Vale of White Horse Hotel, Minety.

The only member of the Hughes family who did not spend much on drink was poor Eder who was the unfortunate one as his mind never fully developed. He never seemed to understand anything connected with keeping a regular job and more or less had to be kept by his brothers. He was quite harmless but did the most unpredictable things and would put himself to work anywhere that came to his mind. A farmer may have got a field of hay "cocked up" into heaps to safeguard it against summer rain and ready to "summer rick" or load on to the waggon and would find on returning to the hayfield poor Eder, his arms full of hay, spreading the hay all around so that it had to be raked up again. He would then ask for a shilling for what he had done. Other times he would go into the fox covers and tear out branches of prickly gorse and lay it in neat rows.

He seemed to have some sort of instinct about the time and would be striding out towards home at nightfall. If asked where he had been he would say perhaps that he had done "Acre and a half of tater digging. All out." Often as he was walking along, both hands in his coat pockets, he would stop suddenly, pick up a loose stone or stick and hurl it into the roadside hedge or without warning turn suddenly and walk straight across the road. One day he dashed across in front of a lorry. Although the driver was taken unawares he was able to slow down but not before he had bumped poor Eder, who was laid out on the road. Out jumped the driver who was to have his second surprise in less than as many minutes. He ran back and asked Eder, "Are you alright mate? Have I hurt you much?" Old Eder had a ready answer. "Couple o' bob'll put it right. Couple o' bob'll put it right." He was not so slow in making certain of a bit of ready cash! That gave the driver something to think about as he proceeded on his journey and no doubt realising he was lucky to have got off so lightly.

When Viv Sutton kept the grocery and bakery business in Silver Street, the yard there became in need of repair, and a load of gravel was delivered and deposited in the yard in the late afternoon and left there until next morning when the work was to be carried out. Imagine Sutton's surprise when he looked out next morning to see the gravel in a tidy heap on the opposite side of the road. Old Eder had chanced along before anyone was about in the early morning, found a shovel, and no doubt thought he was doing a good job of work.

One day, when I was in the garage business with Phil Miles, at Fairfield, on the Malmesbury road, old Eder was going past on one of his "jobs." It was raining in torrents and Phil's dog was lying under a car which was standing at the back of the garage. Old Eder came striding in all dripping wet and stood looking around quite harmlessly, but he had noticed the dog sleeping under the car. Phil came in and asked if we had seen his dog anywhere. Quick as a flash old Eder said, "Ay, thur 'e is, down thur under the chaffcutting machine." He stood there until the time came for us to lock up the garage. Not wanting to offend him I got a sack to put round his shoulders and told him his tea would be cold and off he went without another word.

Of the Hughes family the one I knew best was Fred. He did quite a lot of work for me at one time or another. He was a very good workman and knew as much as most and more than I did about hedging and ditching. Fred was the youngest of the brothers and during World War I he served in France with the Warwicks and then in Italy being in some of the worst of the fighting. The Infantry, nicknamed P.B.I., meaning poor bloody infantry, took the brunt of the fighting and seventeen times poor Fred went over the top with the bayonet. This was a great ordeal for any man so on account of this he was put on "cookhouse" duties, but not before he had contracted "trench foot" caused by being exposed in wet or frozen garments.

He once told me the thing he would never forget was shooting a squirrel in Italy! His Sergeant-Major was going home on leave and wanted to take a pelt home for his wife, so Fred took his rifle. As they were in wooded country, squirrels were common and in plentiful supply. One shot only was needed and the Sergeant-Major was able to get his pelt. Fred's foot gave him trouble for many years and during mealtimes he would take off his boot and wrap it up again before resuming work.

Fred was working for me during World War II as I was reclaiming some derelict land which the Ministry of Agriculture wanted brought into production again. The fields were half-way between Minety and Ashton Keynes and a decoy airfield ran through them.

As there was no shelter in bad weather I towed a large fowl's house along and parked it under one of the hedges. This he made his headquarters. It provided protection from rain or snow. There was plenty of wood available to get a good fire going and old Fred was quite happy to spend a day there working entirely on his own. Perhaps I would not see him for a day or two, but he got on with the job.

They used to tell a good story about old Fred. It was while they were all living at the "Vale." Fred was working at Summerhouse Farm, travelling the one-and-a-half miles there and back on a bicycle. One morning a local resident met Fred on the road walking. Not only walking but walking towards home. "What's the matter then Fred? Aren't you going to work today?" he asked. "Oh aye" said Fred, "but I forgot my dinner and I be late as 'tis." "Where's your bike then?" "Oh, back ther" said Fred, "I left un tiled up against the gate." It hadn't occurred to him to go back on the bicycle!

I am afraid that none of these brothers are living now. I believe old Eder was eventually taken care of in a home for the aged. Abraham lost his life while cutting a hedge beside the Malmesbury road. Having cut back and made a walk between the hedge and the overgrown bushes he apparently set the brush on fire to burn it off. I don't suppose the true story will ever be known but it would seem that his clothes caught fire from a spark and he got entangled in the thorns, away in the fields and alone. He was found later, burnt to death.

*   *   *   *

FOR many years buyers from London came to Swindon Market on Mondays where they bought large quantities of poultry, there being a great demand for

90

them among the Jewish Community. We often took a load of overyeared or nonlaying hens, driving a milk cart with a pig net tied over it and having to leave home in the early morning to be sure of getting them booked in before the auction commenced. Farmers and poultry keepers went through a very difficult period in the twenties and thirties and I remember that a load of old hens would make in auction only tenpence or a shilling each.

Returning from one of these excursions, I had passed the railway bridge at Rushy Platt and was approaching Mannington when I heard a great commotion and much shouting from behind me. On looking round I saw to my consternation a horse at full gallop with a pair of wheels trailing behind. Pulling my horse quickly to one side the horse passed me on the grass verge. At the same time one wheel hitched against a telegraph pole, burst the traces and breeching and away ahead of me the horse disappeared, still going "flat out." The cause of this immediately became apparent when I was able to take another glance behind. The horse had been drawing a four-wheeled vehicle containing four men. The king pin which held the front wheels, undercarriage and shafts had broken. There in the middle of the road, nose down, was the rear half of the carriage and a bunch of men, no doubt bruised and shaken rising to their feet. Having about twelve miles yet to drive, a horse that did not value time as much as I did and an hour or two of milking waiting for me I regret I did not go back to investigate further. Suffice is to say it caused my horse to move a bit faster which was my chief concern. To this day I have never heard who the unfortunate individuals were, but no doubt some of them are still living.

Moss's Corner, Upper Minety.

Stories from Upper Minety

For many years during the latter part of the nineteenth century the house standing near the Oaksey turn on the Minety to Eastcourt road, facing north with large shed abutting on the west side was in fact the Post Office and Shoeing Forge, occupied by the Hinder family for over fifty years. The name of Abraham Hinder is mentioned at that address in Kelly's Directory for 1885 and the family were still living there after 1920.

A story goes that a certain local farmer had been waiting there for a considerable time waiting for his horse to be shod. Fearing that the "Old Inn" would be closed before he could get there he left the Forge in much haste. Mounting his horse, he dug his heels in and set off at a gallop. On the corner opposite was a drockway with wooden railings, two posts with rails extending. The horse being newly-shod stumbled as he was rounding the bend and fell against the end of one of the rails which pierced its chest killing it instantly.

* * * *

On the Oaksey Road, opposite Flistridge Farm, there stood an old thatched cottage where dwelt Mrs. Isabella Humphries and her family. They kept a cow or two which were put to graze in fields down by Rigsby's Lane called the "Ruddocks," formerly the property of the Keenes. However, the fields were sold to Abraham Young Brown, a big landowner at the time, who gave the Humphries' notice to quit, took away the gate which gave access and substituted a stile to prevent the late tenant from turning any cattle through. One night the Humphries' uprooted the stile, turned it bottom upwards so that it was only about two feet high and attached the following notice:—

> *This stile being the property of A. Y. Brown,*
> *We thought we'd turn it upside down,*
> *The Mortgagees could not agree,*
> *So we've made it stand as high as his knee.*

Minety folks had their sense of humour even in those days.

* * * *

FOR many years there was kept in the belfry of St. Leonard's Church a very good set of handbells on leather thongs and ranging two octaves. For a few weeks previous to each Christmas a number of youths, mostly choristers and bellringers, would assemble in the belfry and with the light of oil lamps, candles and torches practice the Christmas carols; the music being set in four parts, treble, alto, tenor and bass on large cards. Then during the week before Christmas we would go round the village playing at as many houses as possible. Often we were entertained with drinks and light refreshments and a donation was put in the hat. The proceeds were traditionally divided up amongst the ringers. Being the recognised practice this was looked forward to with great pleasure by the lads.

I well remember one cold dark night we were making our way back to the Church after a good evening's carolling, old Charlie Packer was in charge being the eldest and also a member of the Church ringers. Getting over a stile where there was a ditch and plank footbridge, old Charlie slipped. The hem of his long overcoat caught on the stile and out shot all our night's takings. I shall never forget how we all groped about in the water in the dark, muddy ditch retrieving pennies and sixpences, until we thought we had salvaged the most of it. I expect there is still some small change in that ditch to this day.

Old Arthur Matthews, alas now no more, used to tell the story of the night they had been calling at several farmhouses and had drunk a quantity of rough cider, then going on to Braydon Hall where Colonel Pim lived at the time. Arthur could not remember what they had to drink there but I am afraid they were no credit to the church when they left, all being more or less "under the influence." Arthur and some others eventually got back as far as the Church Corner where some of them spent the remainder of the night. They had lost most of the handbells. So the first thing in the morning they had to retrace their steps and were fortunate in finding them, but how much of the loose cash was lost was never known. Incidents such as this I am glad to say were rare.

Reads

WHILE I cannot mention every family I have known and remember I think pride of place must be given to the Reads, one of the oldest and most respected families in the village of Minety, who are known to have been living here for at least three hundred years either as tenent or yeoman farmers.

The St. Leonard's Church register has an entry recording "Giles Read. Son of George and Katherine. Born 30th October 1688."

The earliest incident I have to record in connection with the family is a tragedy which occurred in about the middle of the nineteenth century to a Thomas Read, father of William whose family is the main subject of my story. As the story goes, Thomas Read was helping his neighbour, John Brain who farmed at "Isaacs" to get his hay into stack. Apparently the wagon had been loaded. Thomas being loader was on the top and as he pulled on the rope to secure the load it broke and he fell backwards to the ground. They say he was carried into the stable but that he died from his injuries before help could be summoned.

Now William Read, "Grampy" as he was known was a hard working and industrious man and it is to his credit that in spite of the state of agriculture and although he had a family of eighteen children he was able to pay his way and eventually become a land owner. He also managed to get most of his sons started on their own account. I have heard it said that old William Read would mow an acre of grass with a scythe and then get to Malmesbury either on foot or horseback by ten o'clock in the morning. I myself can well remember him and have also known the five generations that have followed. The following list of William Read's children has been given to me by members of the family. . .

Daughters			*Sons*
Elizabeth			Thomas.
Sarah.	Married name Dixon.		Richard.
Thursa.	„	„ Smart.	John. Emigrated to Canada.
Emily.	„	„ Hucks.	George.
Lucy.	Lost her life in a fire.		Ernest. Died aged ten.
Jane.	Married name Foote.		Rowland.
Lucy.	„	„ Keen.	Jonathan.
Liza.	„	„ Ponting.	Edgar. Died in infancy.
Stella	„	„ Miles.	Daniel. Lost his life by being struck in the temple by stone from a catapult, as a boy, while "bird dubbing" on Moor Leaze Farm.

Rowland Read

Of the sons of William, the first I will start with his son Rowland. He attended markets far and near, on one occasion buying a hundred sheep at Salisbury. There was no transport as such at that time and cattle, sheep and pigs were taken on foot by "drovers." Salisbury being at a distance of something like fifty miles away it took sometimes several days to cover the journey which the drover had to break at nightfall. He would turn the sheep into a field and sleep under the hedge to start away first thing in the morning. To his surprise he found one morning that he had turned them into a large field where there was another flock and had great difficulty in parting them up. As this was away on the Downs with no houses near he was unable to get any help, so he decided he would make the best of a bad job, but at least he would be sure of getting his hundred.

Counting and recounting during the day he found that he had about one hundred and six. So when he eventually arrived home he asked his master, Rowland, just how many he was supposed to have. When told "one hundred" he said, suppose there's over one hundred, can I have 'em?" To which the reply was "Yes." The sheep were counted again and there were six over. These were forthwith sent to the local market and the proceeds duly transferred to the drover's pocket. How often this sort of thing took place luckily history does not record.

Rowland's eldest son Frank was one of the first men I ever saw riding a motor cycle. That was long enough before World War I.

Thomas Read

Now Thomas Read, besides being Farmer and Butcher was also the Carrier to Cirencester, driving an old pony and trap. The story goes that one morning he was hitching up his pony when old Lewis Slade came striding down Sawyer's Hill at the foot of which was Thomas Read's house "Frogmore." His old pony was never a fast mover, a fact of which Lewis Slade was well aware. However, Thomas Read was a good natured sort of fellow and shouted out to Slade, "Would you like a lift? I'm just going to 'Ciren'." "Ah, Thanks all the same" says Slade. "I think I'd better walk. I'm in a hurry" and away he went stepping a "good yard."

Very often when Thomas went to town he would have so many calls to make that it made a long day for him and he would have to drive home at night by lamplight. The old trap lamps were made for candles in long sockets underneath with a coil spring to keep the candle moving upwards in position as it burnt down. However, on one occasion after a very long day, his candle burnt out before he had reached home. Arriving home in the dark, knowing his way around pretty well he was able to unhitch the horse, unharness it and turn it loose in the paddock.

His wife, as was usual on such occasions had gone to bed and left a basin of broth on the "hob" to keep warm for him. Thomas, after groping about in the dark eventually found his supper which he greedily consumed and was soon in bed and fast asleep. His wife, going down first in the morning, noticed the basin of broth untouched. So she shouted up the stairs, "Thomas, why didn't ye yet thee supper last night?" Thomas called back "I did yet me supper." At this his wife was rather concerned and went back to the hob to have another look. "Lawks, Lawks, Thomas!" cries she. "If thee hasn't yeten be basin of starch and bonnet strings." "Well, well!" says Thomas. "I thought the cabbage was main tough."

At one time Thomas was on the Parish Council and was once said to have declared, "It's my opinion as 'e may term't, that in years to come there will be a great scarcity of water, as such a large amount goes off in steam."

While on the subject of water, Thomas' nephew, also Thomas by name, and a pretty dry old stick, was discussing the water problem at Minety after it had been decided to put the village on the mains under a new Council scheme. Minety, as every inhabitant knows is a very wet place and when the news was given to Thomas junior his remark was "I don't know so much about laying the water on. I should think it's about time some of it was 'laid off'."

It should go on record here that three of the Read brothers, Thomas, Richard and George married three sisters by the name of Ponting, Adelaide, Louisa and Frances respectively. So it goes without saying that the two families are very closely knit, also very much in character, being by and large, a real good old-fashioned "honest to goodness" type of Wiltshire countryfolk, generally industrious and enterprising, and today are very firmly established in this part of the County. Of the two families, if there is anything to choose between them, perhaps the Ponting side are if anything a trifle more ardent supporters of the Brewery companies. But both families are very loyal patrons and usually manage to get to the local before it is all gone.

George Read

George worked up quite a large Pork business, sometimes handling as many as sixty pigs a day. Although carried on by his sons they were put out of business when during the 1939–45 War the Government zoned all the Meat Trade, closing down local butchers and distributing all meat from Central Abbatoirs, this area coming under Swindon. The farm was still carried on with a reduced staff. Although George bought a number of pigs at local markets he also purchased quite a lot from local farmers. He usually walked on his buying expeditions wearing a mackintosh and Trilby hat turned down, walking stick crooked on his arm and thumbs stuck in his braces or the armholes of his waistcoat. He danced along with a springy gait, toes outward pointing so you could recognise him a mile away.

He called on me one day when I had eight good porkers in a sty and without me putting a price to them he offered me "three pounds apiece" for them. It so happened that one of them had not come to the trough that morning. So I said "I'm sorry Mr. Read, I cannot sell them to you today. One of them was off its feed this morning." Within a week I had lost six of the eight with Pluero Pneumonia. That's how things go with farming. On another occasion I had a cow which was very wild and would kick like a mule. The only thing I could do was to sell her to the butcher.

One evening some grass keep was being auctioned adjoining Rudge Lane and George Read came on foot using the footpath across my Farm. As we approached the milking herd I told George that I had a fresh barrener and asked him if he could do with her. We stopped half-way across the field and I pointed the cow out to him. She seemed to know that we were discussing her and turned round and held her head up like a giraffe! That was enough for George. He just said "Ah, I counts 'er wouldn't be much good to I Varmer." So I had to market her. I walked her to Cricklade at the time the market was held in the High Street, the auctioneer's rostrum being under the clock by the Vale Hotel. Augustus Hart and Tom Ferris doing most of the auctioning. I was dreading the moment I should have to drive my cow into the ring as I fully expected her to charge across and jump over the rails into the crowd. Then to my utter amazement a neighbour of mine, Benjamin Greenslade, being at the ringside, she quietly walked in and started licking his coat sleeve, standing there until the bidding had ceased, and she was sold for about £17, half the price I had paid for her. But I was very relieved to see the back of her.

As I remarked previously, three of old Grampy William Read's sons married three sisters named Ponting whose father was then farming at Braydon. There were not even bicycles in those days and most of the journeys to visit the girls were made on foot. It was quite common to walk six miles and back of an evening. One night George Read had been to Braydon, came back over Minety Pike and Silver Street and was approaching Sawyer's Hill. It was a quiet night and very late, and just as he was about opposite Field House he heard what sounded like a lot of little pigs squealing and a terrific scratching of feet on the road. It has often been said that rats move by night in whole droves and I have often noticed in farming that sometimes you are overrun by rats and suddenly they seem to disappear. As he stood in the road wondering what was the cause of the noise, all at once the road was black with rats scampering and squealing, and seeing him standing in the road, they all turned off and disappeared down what is known as Chapel Lane. I have never experienced such a thing, but it bears out the fact and I have no reason to disbelieve this story. I did however several years ago see a tremendous flight of starlings, which some books say are seen all the year round while others say they migrate to the Continent of Europe. Whichever is the case they do move around in very large flocks. Several years ago, standing under an apple tree in my orchard which adjoins a field, the "Homeground," six acres in extent, I saw what appeared to be a dark cloud approaching. On closer observation it turned out to be an enormous flock of birds. After circling round they pitched in the Homeground apparently covering every square inch so that the whole field was absolutely black with starlings. There must have been several millions. After twittering around for a few moments they just as suddenly flew off in a northerly direction.

Some authorities affirm that while the starling is a resident bird in this country they are reinforced by huge flocks which migrate from Northern Europe. As these were flying north they may have been some of these.

Pork was George Read's chief line and at one time he supplied as many as twenty butchers in Swindon. Much of the pork he delivered by road, in later years by motor van. Much of it went to Smithfield Market and this was sent by rail in special vans in which it was suspended, one van taking forty or more pigs.

Calves of which he was also a buyer were often sent live by rail in calf crates, holding six to eight calves each, mounted on four wooden wheels. They were taken by wagon to the railway station, wheeled on to the trucks or vans and the wheels then removed.

As a judge of pigs I doubt if he was ever surpassed. One look over the pigsty wall or the pen in the market and he knew their value. He was a familiar figure for many years at the local markets from Andoversford to Swindon, including Cirencester, Cricklade, Malmesbury, Wootton Bassett and Tetbury. Two of his sons who were brought up in the business often had to buy for him to satisfy the demand for pork and veal. For many years he was called on at shows and Christmas Fat Stock Markets to judge the pigs and his judgement could seldom if ever be criticised. He was able to find employment for all his four sons and son-in-law and three or four men besides to help with the slaughtering and dressing. Several of his grandsons were also employed until World War II when the Ministry of Food closed down so many businesses and required all meat to be dealt with at Central Abbatoirs. Three of his sons served in World War I, Frank, the eldest being killed in action.

George Read, like most children of that generation left school at the age of eleven or twelve years to help his father in the butchery business, old William carrying on the business of Pork Butcher as well as farming the Moor Leaze Farm. George frequently accompanied his father to the markets when he was old enough and often had to walk back with a herd of pigs or cattle there being no transport as there is today.

To the casual observer, looking at a bunch of pigs or cattle or a flock of sheep you learn very little of their nature or habits. For instance, when driving a bunch of pigs on a highway, from some instinctive notion and for reasons which are quite obscure to you they will suddenly stop and refuse to be driven any further. They have noticed something that you haven't, perhaps a railway bridge or some other unfamiliar object and will turn and bolt as fast as they can in the opposite direction and it may be half an hour before you can get them together and on the trot again. With sheep it is almost uncanny. If you tried to drive them from a field or fold you might shout and wave your arms or even put the dog on them and all they will do is go round in a circle. But just grab one by the fleece and carry it through the gateway and the others will follow immediately. One sheep will never leave the flock of its own accord.

With cattle they will usually keep together. There may be trouble at cross roads or when passing open gates and most often there is one in the bunch that is determined to go back the way it came. So you can realise the trials and tribulations that beset the cattle drover.

To go back to my story, when George Read was a boy he went from Minety to Calne Market where his father bought a bunch of pigs. Young George had to walk them back to Minety a distance of nearly twenty miles. How long the journey took will never be known but eventually after getting through Brinkworth and Somerford Common he came to the cross roads by the house which was once a beer house known as the "Blue Pig". He had had enough trouble already but when he got here the pigs went off in all four directions as fast as they could go. Poor George was so overcome he just sat down and cried. I sometimes wonder how some of the present generation would react in such circumstances.

Jonathan Read

Jonathan Read was the youngest of the sons of William, being born on the day that the Franco-Prussian War broke out in 1870. Besides writing verse he also produced a play, a farce really, which was called "Rustic Loyalty." This play was actually produced at the Empire Theatre, Swindon, and caused quite a stir at the time. Jonathan was quite a character and it is related that on one occasion, on being told that he wanted a haircut, his reply was "All poets have long hair."

Now Jonathan Read was prepared to try anything to make a shilling. At one time he got hold of an old magic lantern complete with glass "slides," and then advertised the "Show" on the public notice boards. The night arrived and Jonathan was there in good time to get his apparatus fixed up.

However, it turned out a very bad night in more ways than one for Jonathan, being very rough and wet. When the time for the show to commence came there was only one person in the audience sitting at the back. Undismayed, he made his well-rehearsed introductory speech, describing some of his pictures from all over the world, including a close-up of Niagara Falls. This, incidentally, he exhibited upside down.

Johnathan Read.
Farmer, Publican, Poet, Playwright.

Still undaunted by the very small attendance Jonathan concluded by announcing "Ladies and Gentlemen, although as you will have noticed we have a very small audience, so as not to disappoint you I intend going through the entire programme." Up gets the old fellow at the back and shouts out "Hurry up and get it over with then boss. I wants to lock up!" Whether this is authentic I am not prepared to say. Perhaps in this case a grain of salt may be advisable.

Jonathan also taught one of his sons to walk a tightrope, which feat he would perform at the local shows, carrying a tray on which stood a glass of beer. I never once saw him come to grief.

A SELECTION OF POEMS BY JOHNATHAN READ

Song of A Prisoner in the Transvaal

Comrades just bear a moment with me
And hear my song though absent I roam
Though daring enemies surround me,
My mind still sees the fireplace at home.

> *Chorus:*
> At Home, yes at Home,
> My heart lingers there
> Where parents and friends
> Plead for me in Prayer.

Our soldier's coat hides a mutual heart
True to his country, true to his own,
Fighting for victory, thinking of home
Three days, yet a smile drives back the frown.

> *Chorus:*
> Now with his leader, a prisoner he
> Quietly smiles as they lead him away,
> For he knows there's a Queen who will see
> That all her subjects will have fair play.

Contentment

A Gem, a Guiding Star which casts its beams
Around me, to warm my troubled thoughts by
Its endearing rays, sets fears and cares aside
And imbues my soul with thankfulness.
A Tree that shadeth from the rays of a
Burning wrath, casts drops of dew to damp the
Smothering fire that is almost alight,
And cool me down to know myself, and so
Repent my haste. What Diamond can be more
Precious? What Sapphire more rare? Contentment!

Piety

The elements clash with thunder round
The frail barque of Life.
To fright a weakness with its sound
And keep me from the strife.

But thunder's clash to music turns
When heart cries "I am free."
Within this breast true fire burns
Of Meekness, Piety.

Death of Prince Henry of Battenburg

Two suns have shone from out one genial sky,
Together rose and cheered each other's way,
And strewn with flowers the craggy rocks of life
To smooth the hillside of each other's pain.
Together smiled away the surging tide
Of griefs and cares, with one white-robed content.

One sun has set, a trembling silver light
Sheds round its vacant seat a liquid glare
Of brightness, leading to a place of rest,
And dries the filial eyes of crowding fears,
Calms down the stricken heart with a soothing
Close entwining hope, a love's sweet content.

The other sun is shaded with a cloak
.... rents sad crushing care, millions
of kindred stars shoot here and there, in one
Gold bond of sympathy, to polish o'er
The darkened spot of grief's last cruel touch.
Bring back that sacred smile, our land's content.

Richard Read

Continuing my stories of the Read family, Richard was rather a sedate type, a very regular Churchman, walking to Morning Service as a ritual, up through the Lower Moor, under the Railway Bridge, skirting the Laines, up Windmill and through the Green. He was usually accompanied by three of his daughters, Ben Greenslade and myself and a lively conversation ensued all the way. Old Richard always sat against the North wall five or six pews from the back, and although I am writing this in 1970 and he died in the twenties, there is still the round indent on the wall where he used to rest his head, eyes closed during the Sermons. Short and stocky in build and of a happy disposition, he was said to have been a very good athlete in his younger days, as were most of his family, he could put up a bar, walk under it, then turn round and jump over it—no mean feat. At one time the Read family could field a whole team in either cricket or football, they provided some of the best talent in the Minety Clubs, one of them actually having a trial for Swindon Town Football Club.

Richard could often be heard singing as he drove about the village or worked on his farm, often sitting on his cart load of corn or meal. His favourite song ran thus:—

> "I used to take her everywhere
> To all the sights around,
> But now she's left me in despair,
> Naughty Jemima Brown."

William Keen

Of the family of seventeen of William Read of Moor Leaze Farm, one daughter, Lucy, married a master builder and carpenter by the name of William Keen who had retired from the successful business he had carried on in London. He bought a house in the lower Moor with five or six acres of pasture and a large orchard. He built a good stable and trap house, kept a useful pony and four-wheeled conveyance and did quite a lot of driving around the countryside. Periodically he and his wife would make the journey to London by easy stages staying a night or two at a wayside pub or hostelry if necessary, starting off again in the morning. Surely this must be the most enjoyable way of taking a holiday.

William Keen was anything but a farmer but having married into a farming family he was much in their company and listening to conversation about farming problems of which he knew very little. It appears that one of them had a cow with udder trouble, a common ailment which in this case left the owner with a "Three quartered" cow. Now William was mystified by this and when he got home he asked his wife "Lucy, what do they mean when they say a cow has lost a quarter?" "Why", says she, "it means it does not give any milk on one of its teats." "Well

I'm demmed" replied William, "I thought it must have lost a leg or something."
When the First World War came he offered his services to the War Ministry and
went to Salisbury Plain erecting huts for Army Authorities.

Oliver Read

At least eleven Reads served in World War I, all grandsons of William, besides
sons-in-law of George, Thomas and Heber Smart, many of them schoolmates of
mine. Alas, the two brothers Smart were both killed, Tom serving with the Canadians and Heber with the Royal Field Artillery. George Read's other two sons
survived the war; Frank was killed, William going into the coal business at Purton,
whilst Oliver came back to the Butchery business. Always a great sportsman he
played football and cricket for Minety for many years. He was a great organiser
and was responsible for scores of char-a-banc outings for local organisations. He
was very versatile and fond of a good joke. Not to be outdone by his Uncle
Johnathan the Poet he actually ventured on a poem singing the praises of Minety
Football Club. Copies of this were printed by Taylor's Printing Works before
World War I in which at least three of the team lost their lives—Ernest Burdock,
Bill (William) Vizer and George Garland.

This poem, singing the praises of Minety Football Club, the only poem I know
of from the pen of Oliver Read, I consider worth recording, not only for its originality but also for the fact that it reflects sport, and football in particular as it was
played in the "good old days." I set it down here with the full consent of the author.

Minety Football Club
Written by OLIVER READ, who played for Minety, 1910 onwards

> Hurrah for Minety Football Club
> And Mark Jones keeps up the rub.
> With "Minety House" of ancient fame,
> Headquarters of the pop'lar game.
>
> Minety opens with a win
> And twice they sent the ball right in.
> Let's give the Tetbury team their due
> But never once could they get through.
>
> Yes, they had boasted o'er and o'er
> That they'd beat Minety by the score.
> Hark! The loud "O. Read" plays today.
> Come Tetbury! buck up, shew your play.
>
> In goal, H. Bunce stops attacks
> Bill Vizer and E. Burdock, backs,
> Freddy Read and O. Read too
> With G. Garland, are half-backs true.
>
> Sam Canter playing Inside right
> Can kick the ball right out of sight
> King Read in the forward line
> Secured two goals by shooting fine.
>
> Arthur Burdock and George Freeth
> Can still their situation keep.
> Mark Jones, a worthy forward too
> Really ought to have got through.
>
> Now they have played again. By Gum!
> And won their second match 2–1
> Brinkworth United were second placed
> Defeated, yet were not disgraced.

100

Brains

IN the 1870's there farmed at Gibbs Farm old John Brain, who, being a very hard drinker and having three large orchards, always made plenty of rough cider. For many years and even until quite recently the Cider Mill travelled around from farm to farm, each farmer sending a horse and man to fetch the outfit from the last user and providing his own labour to work it. Quite a number of men were required and were collected locally, each farmer helping his neighbour. The apples were brought to the Mill in sacks by the wagon load. One man would be fully occupied tipping them into a bushel basket and then into the mill to be ground and crushed, the pulp falling into a long trough from which it was shovelled to the men filling the press. The pulp was wrapped in large horsehair cloths, laid in a box about two feet square and turned over into the press. It took six of these to fill the press which was firmly pegged to the ground. A long iron screw projected from the top of the mill which was turned by means of thick wooden poles socketed into the hub. Attached to the base of the screw was a large slab of board which pressed down squeezing the apple juice out. This was bucketed out of the trough into waiting barrels usually set on the wagon to save having to lift them when full. One man carried the buckets of cyder, another standing on the wagon to do the filling. It took four men when available to turn the hand operated mill, one handle on each side and two men to a handle. This was nicknamed the "Joywheel" and we were always glad to have a rest from it by helping to screw the press. As the press was screwed down, more pressure was required and this was obtained by inserting long iron bars into the screw sockets and four or five men operating it with a jerking movement until there was a danger of the whole thing bursting or being wrenched out of the ground. Every last drop of juice was pressed out. There was always a plentiful supply of old cyder to quench the thirst of the workers. When the pulp had been squeezed dry, the pressure was taken off, the cloths taken out, the contents emptied into a heap and the process repeated. Often the "pugs" as the dry pulp was called was fed to pigs.

As the day wore on the jokes and jests became more rowdy and it was the recognised thing for at least one or two of the gang to become pretty unsteady on their feet by nightfall.

George Brain, known as "Peggy."

101

This cider was the downfall of poor old John Brain. His sons too learned their lesson well and were as expert as he in tipping the mug so that the farm soon passed into other hands. Of his three sons, William, George and John, George followed most closely his father's example. Having no schooling, as a small boy young George would be sent up to the field to walk round the small patch of wheat which it was the custom to grow for bread, bird scaring, by beating an old tin or bucket. This he had to do day after day during the summer months and he told me that he often wandered off, his father having to search for him. He would then be afraid to go indoors for fear of getting a beating and would spend the night in the carthouse, lying in the bed of the cart. Having to give up the farm George was forced to spend his time when necessity demanded working for neighbouring farmers. He was a good worker as long as he was sober, but usually had to be supplied with a gallon jar of cider so that more often than not he was "laid out" by the end of the day. An inveterate poacher he always had a good dog and a single barelled shot gun, 12-bore, and so was able to provide himself with a certain amount of food, most of his earnings going on drink. He had a poor opinion of such games as Football and one Saturday seeing my brother Harry changed for a match he said to him "I dwon't know what thee canst see in kicking that ball about." "Well," says Harry, "that's our sport. Now if you want a bit of sport you have a walk round the fields with your gun and dog. That's your sport." "Ah well!" says George, "that's different. That's zummat for the guts!"

George Brain: "Howse the grass coming on varmer?"
Farmer Brown (who always wears his trousers on rather a slack rein): "Oh! Wonderful. I got grass in the wum ground up to my arse."
George Brain: "Dost thee mean 'up to thy arse' or 'up to the arse o' thee trousers?'"

He was a dry old character in some respects. Usually on Sunday mornings after taking his walk round the fields with his gun and dog he would call in at the Moor Farm for a drink of cider to round it off. Sometimes he would have a companion as many like to have a walk on a Sunday morning, sit on a gate or a stile and tell a few yarns. On one particular Sunday George encountered Richard Read's son Arthur so they strolled along together as far as Swillbrook and the Pye Ends. Just across the Brook in a very isolated cottage lived an old man named Bowley who kept a few ducks. These ducks loved the brook where there was good pickings for them.

Old George said nothing as the ducks enjoyed themselves, stretching their necks to the bottom of the brook, quite content with the world in general. However, George and Arthur eventually decided it was time to gently start wending their way homeward. Sitting on a gate for a few minutes before setting off George says to Arthur "Do'st thee want a duck you?" "What do'st thee mean?" says Arthur. "Oh, one o' they ducks down on the brook" replies George. "Oh no," says Arthur, "our old chap would beat the daylights out of I if I took one of them home." "Oh well," says George, "If thee bisn't gwine to 'ave one, I Be!" With that he turned to his well-trained poacher's dog and says "Go on you! Go and get one." The old dog up and away over the bank, into the brook and was back in a flash with a duck between its jaws. Old George took the duck, pulled its neck, turned to Arthur and says, "Theest might as well have one theest know." "That's as may be," says Arthur, "but its more than I darest do to take one o' they home." "Oh well, please theeself. If thee bisn't goin' to have one I might as well have thine." And away went the old dog for another.

At that time old George was living in a one-roomed cottage with his brother John. They took it in turn to cook the Sunday dinner which usually consisted of mixed vegetables and perhaps a piece of bacon boiled up in an old pot hanging over a wood fire. One Sunday when it was John's turn, being somewhat lazy or perhaps sleeping off the after-effects of the previous night's booze-up he was late getting the pot on. Old George returning from a long walk and feeling pretty hungry had a suspicion that the dinner was not cooked, lifted the lid. The potatoes had only just been put in. He grabbed the handle of the pot and slung the dinner, pot and all, out of the door on to the garden. "If that's the best thee can do, in future thee get thy dinner and I'll get mine," said he. And so I suppose that's how it had to be.

As I have said before, old George was a good worker when sober, hedge cutting, ditching, thatching, and one of his specialities was pig killing. Most farmers fatted a pig for the household about once a year, killed and cured it by salting the sides for about three weeks, then with a string and a peg, hanging it against a wall to dry or laying it on a rack hung from the ceiling. This was just old George's handwriting as he was always allowed a piece of pigmeat and perhaps some of the chitterlings or inwards. For many years he was known to all and sundry as "Piggy Brain," pronounced "Peggy Brain" in these parts. An event which happened when I was a child will always stand out in my memory. "Peggy" was about to slaughter a pig for Abel Garland, the hurdle maker in Silver Street. Three or four men were holding the pig down on the bench for him, the pig squealing as only a pig can, when down the street came Miss Bushby, step-daughter of Captain James who then lived at Braydon Hall, leading a massive bulldog. The bulldog streaked away from Miss Bushby, grabbed the pig and was actually dragging it down the yard away from its captor until she had to lay into it with the heavy dog whip which she always carried when exercising it. It was some time before equilibrium could be restored and unfortunately for the pig, the slaughter completed.

Old George seemed to possess a natural sense of humour which soon became evident to all who came into contact with him, although many of his jokes were at the expense of the unfortunate individual who inspired him to some amusing and very often personal remark.

It is indeed a fact that up until fifty years ago or so elderly people appeared much older than they would today with the advantage of such things as good dental treatment. The majority of old people had no teeth at all or just a few odd ones here and there so that when the mouth was closed chin and nose came into very close contact. Also I recollect there seemed to be a far greater number of people who over the years either as a result of their labours or through some accident had become permanently bent, having to walk with a stick, in a stooping position their eyes glued to the ground except for an occasional twist of the head for navigational purposes. They were and are much to be pitied for this affliction but there was no sentimentality or pity to be got from old George Brain. At that time there lived in an old cottage in London Lane, still standing, an elderly man named Henry South-wood. Almost fifty per cent of Minety then consisted of allotments, one such being between Woodward's Farm and the Purleius.

On one particular evening a number of men were there busily occupied tilling or cultivating their strips, among them old George Brain. Poor Southwood who was truly a man to be pitied having developed a very bad stoop appeared on the scene. George looked up from his hoeing and says in a very serious voice, "Hast thee come straight from home, Southwood?" "Aye, Aye", answered Southwood. "Well," said George, "If that's the case thee'st got pretty doubled up since thee started."

The trouble with old George was that he was nearly as often drunk as sober, the public houses in those days being open all day. Towards the end of his career although he became unsteady on his legs he still continued to drink. He was on the top of a hayrick one day just placing the final pitch of hay to the point of the roof when he lost his balance and fell to the ground. How many bones he broke will never be known. They got him home somehow to the almshouse in the Moor where he was then living, but he never saw a doctor. He laid on an old sofa downstairs for some weeks, one and another taking in food and an occasional bottle of cyder. He eventually got on his feet again and returned to the old one-roomed cottage he had previously shared with his brother, now dead. George always wore a red handkerchief around his neck instead of a tie, shirt unbuttoned. After the death of his eldest brother Bill he was cutting some hedge for my father, and I walked across the field where he was working to fodder some cattle it being winter time. I noticed that he was wearing a new handkerchief and asked, "You going to old Bill's funeral then George?" "Noa," said he. "What's the good of looking after they as be dead? 'E wants to look after they as be a livin'." He was not breaking his heart over a thing like that.

His end was very tragic really. His old cottage was condemned and he was notified by the Council that he would have to go to the "Workhouse." We all tried to save the situation for him, even writing to the Press. Being a farmer's son he felt it was beneath his dignity to end his days like this. So George went to a cousin of mine, Henry Lewis, who gave him permission to build a sectional shed on a spare piece of his land between Sawyer's Hill and Askew Bridge. He was expecting his hut to arrive any day and was walking along to look over the site. He had not got very far before he fell down in a state of collapse. Passers-by carried him to the carpenter's shop used by William Morgan nearby but poor old George had breathed his last. The irony of it was that the hut arrived on that very day on a lorry which passed by on the road as he lay dead. It had, of course to be sent back without him even seeing it. With the passing of old George one of the greatest links with the past was severed. I only wish I could remember half the stories he told me over the years.

Beames—A George Brain Story

IN my younger days it was the rule rather than the exception that there should be a barrel of cider in the house. Whether farmhouse or cottage apples were grown practically everywhere and what were known as "crab apples" could be found growing in the hedgerows. Although money was scarce it should not be forgotten that Public Houses were allowed to keep open all day and beer was only a penny or twopence a pint. Agricultural workers were able to get cider apples very cheaply or even have them given to them by their employers and cider was the main drink for almost everyone. Made as it was in those days from pure apple juice when properly "doctored" or fermented it was a very potent liquor. The consequence of this was that it was quite a common sight to see a man stretched out on the roadside sleeping off the effects before presenting himself to his wife which otherwise would have led to trouble. If driving a horse and trap there was usually someone at hand to help him into his seat, the rest of the journey being taken care of by the horse which was thankful to make for home anyway having probably been tethered to a ring in the ground at the "local" for several hours and no doubt would have given one of its hind legs for a drink of water.

Old Billy Beames, smallholder and meal merchant was often somewhat the worse for drink and after eventually arriving home unable to get down from his trap. After a time his wife had had just about enough of this. So, one night he came driving into the yard and the horse came to a halt. Out came his wife, unbuckled the breeching and traces, gave the horse a good slap on the rump whereupon it jumped forward, the old lady "up" with the shafts and out pitches old Billy over the back of the cart on his head. How often this happened is not recorded but I have no doubt it had the desired effect and sobered him up somewhat. This drastic treatment was at least one solution to the problem and would no doubt be described today as a "major operation."

The Old Irishman

DURING the first decade or so of the twentieth century there were many homeless men tramping around wandering from place to place finding seasonal work. No doubt many of them were navvies who had been employed on the building of the Railways or cutting of canals, while others may have been deserters from the army. These were often the type who took their first shilling to the "pub" and only worked as a final resort. Some came as cattle drivers from Gloucester or Chippenham, Devizes, Swindon, or Salisbury, hanging around, sleeping in cowsheds in winter and under hedges during the summer, earning just enough to keep themselves in bread and cheese and beer or cyder.

One such character, an Irishman, travelled North Wiltshire, Gloucestershire and Oxfordshire for many years, though no-one seemed to know where he originally hailed from. When sober he was an extremely good worker. When on the road he carried the whole of his belongings in two sacks with a rope tied to the bottom, brought up under the arms and twisted and knotted at the shoulder, one each side, the ropes crossing in front of his body. He wore any old boots with strips of rag wrapped around his feet for "socks", usually two jackets and trousers tied beneath the knees with string, cap on the back of his head. Often he could be heard approaching singing in a beautiful falsetto voice, several days growth of beard upon his face. When sober and clean-shaven he was a remarkably likeable looking fellow, often with a wonderful smile on his face. But once he had a shilling in his pocket he would find some excuse to "pack up" when he would make for the nearest pub. The next you saw of him he would be on the roadside opposite the farmhouse, all his accoutrements scattered around him on the ground, and he, standing in the middle as long as he could keep his balance, cursing everything and everybody within sight. His vocabulary was terrific. Never short of a word he would sometimes keep this up for an hour or two. Having got it off his chest he would pack his bags again and disappear from sight. Nothing more would be either seen or heard of him for several months when he would reappear, singing down the road just as though nothing had happened and offering to do a job or two of work again.

What his real name was no-one seemed to know. In some localities he was known as "Happy Jack" and in others "Irish Jack." If asked, he was evasive and would sometimes say "Oliva—Oliva Tremble—born in a manger." That he had served in the Inniskillen Fusiliers was more than possibly true, though whether he had been a deserter was questionable. It was very evident that he had received Infantry training, as often when "armed" with a yard broom or a hayfork, he would jump to attention and either "slope" or "present arms" with a sly twinkle in his eye. He was a wonderful fellow and had many skills. He would collect oak apples and fir cones, thread them on wire, and using discarded cigar boxes from the public houses for the seats, fashion them into ornamental miniature armchairs about ten

The Old Irishman.
Known as "Happy Jack" or "Old Oliver."

to twelve inches high, selling them for 3d., 4d. or 6d. each. He would also dig up fern roots from roadside banks which he peddled from door to door.

Another special line was to make good hardwearing "mops" with a four-inch wire nail, a leather washer cut from an old boot and a number of squares of cloth. These he sold to housewives for a few pence. All that was needed was a stick for a handle and there they had a very serviceable mop.

In the mangel hoeing season "Old Jack" would invariably be found either on the Cotswolds or in Berkshire or Oxfordshire. On one occasion when he called at the farm of my wife's grandfather to give a hand with this tedious chore he was given the job of "singling out". This is where each row is taken separately and the plants thinned out to about a foot apart thus ensuring good sized roots which were later pulled by hand. They are then cleaned and "topped" of their green leaves, thrown into a temporary heap and the leaves spread over to give protection from the weather. For winter storage the mangels and swedes were carted to a "clamp"— an oblong shaped heap about five feet high and up to fifty yards long, again covered with leaves, a trench dug round and the soil thrown over the "clamp" for protection from frost or rain.

After an acquaintanceship of over thirty years I last saw the old Irishman sitting beside the Lechlade to Bampton road, all his goods and chattels spread around him, looking as happy as a "sandboy." I felt bound to pull up and have a word with him, giving him a sixpence which was enough for him to get drunk on at that time. He had aged considerably and I have heard since that he died soon after and was buried at Chipping Norton. Such "old-timers" as this will never be seen again as long as any form of civilisation remains. They are gone for ever. Here I will mention that the vehicle I was driving on that day was one of the old "Bull-nosed" Morris' with dickey seat, my passenger my uncle, Charles Stratford who was a qualified Master Farrier and Shoeing Smith, son of a Blacksmith, Farrier and General Ironworker of Castle Eaton.

Walkers

BEING of old Wiltshire stock myself it is not but to be expected that I should look around the Braydon Country when in search of a wife and eventually ally myself to a certain Mabel Lilian Walker, whose family have farmed in the Braydon district for many generations, Great grandfather George, Grandfather James and my father-in-law another George. They are listed in the Directory for 1874 and two others, an Edgar Walker and a William have their names on the Voters' List for the parish of Minety in 1887 as occupiers of houses and land on Minety Common.

Now although his father and grandfather were content to follow agricultural pursuits in this country, young George, my wife's father had more ambitious ideas, and as a friend of his had decided to try his luck in Canada, George agreed to go also. He soon found himself a job on a large arable farm and worked alongside his employer's son. Unfortunately they did not get on too well together and this state of affairs was soon brought to a head. The old farmer had sent these two ahead with horse teams to some land away from the homestead where they were to stay overnight ready to start work the following day when the farmer himself was coming to get them started.

Having spent the night in the barn the farmer's son told George to get up and get the kettle on and get him some breakfast. To this George replied "I don't take orders from you and if you want any breakfast do the same as I and get your own." Words led to blows and after a general punch-up young George had his opponent lying in rather a sorry state on the floor.

Expecting the boss to arrive any time and being somewhat battered about the face himself he decided he had best clear off. So, tying a handkerchief round his face he sallied forth and sure enough he had not gone far before he met the farmer who asked him where he was going. "Oh dear" says George, "I've had ramping tooth-ache all night. I shall have to go and have this tooth out before I can do anything" and away he goes as quick as he could before the old farmer found out the real reason for his sudden departure, and soon put as many miles as he could between them.

This seems to have dampened George's ardour for farming and as the Canadian Pacific Railway were laying a line from east to west he joined up with a railway gang, a motley crowd of many nationalities, mostly Canadians with French, Swedes, etc. but very few from the Mother Country. So George became known as "English" by name.

As the nature of the work meant they were constantly moving westwards the men were accommodated in railway vans and as is so often unfortunately the case there was continual discontent among the workers, and George, being a strong burly fellow, the foreman had him to share his van as a sort of bodyguard, relations between employer and employed being in rather a seething state.

However, the situation had been kept under control, or so it was believed, until late one night George and his boss awoke to find the van full of smoke. During the night the men had set it on fire and they had to jump for it with only what they could carry out. So once again young George had to disappear in haste. After this he must have become disillusioned with the idea of any future in Canada and it was not long before he arrived back home a sadder, poorer and wiser man.

107

As the family had left the Braydon country by this time it was to Buscot Wick Farm that he returned. His wanderings over he settled down on his father's farm, married and brought up a family of three sons and five daughters of which I was the lucky man to have first choice for a wife.

Gipsies

A FAMILIAR SIGHT to us in the early part of the century was the gipsy caravans as they moved around the countryside from one encampment to another, sometimes singly, in twos or perhaps half a dozen. All were gaily painted, most of them with the mother sitting on the front seat and numerous children looking out from the inside while the menfolk would be in charge of the horses. Younger women would be calling from door to door carrying large baskets of domestic articles for sale.

The largest encampment that I can remember in this district was on Lydiard Plain, between Purton and Wootton Bassett. There they could be seen sitting round their camp fire, boiling their pots and kettles, busy making baskets and clothes pegs from hazel or willow, whichever was most easily obtainable. The clothes pegs were clipped to strips of wood and found a ready sale at a few pence a dozen.

This was then open common land and still partly covered with gorse bushes. The gipsies occupied many such camping sites throughout the country, mostly on common land but when the 1914-18 war came and food became short, most of this land was taken over under emergency war measures and the gipsies ordered to vacate.

Lydiard Plain was taken over by Wootton Bassett Rural District Council after the war and the gipsies lost their right to camp there. The land was cleared, ploughed and planted with wheat and other crops to help keep the country from starvation.

The gipsies however, undaunted, began to drift back. In a cottage overlooking the Plain lived a man named Bert Gleed, and he, I have been told, was paid the sum of ten pounds per year to notify the police whenever a caravan pulled in.

I understand the Commoners have now lost their rights to graze this land as of old and that it is let yearly by the Wootton Bassett Rural District Council.

Hawkers, Pedlars, etc.

IN this modern age the old-time pedlar or hawker is almost a thing of the past. At one time a man and his wife, perhaps a child or two, would be calling from door to door selling brushes, baskets, pots and pans and all kinds of domestic articles. Sometimes he would be pushing a barrow or truck, sometimes carrying his wares in a large basket but often with a horse or pony drawing a loaded two or four-wheeled conveyance. They had often made such things as brushes and clothes pegs themselves and depended on the sale of these for their living.

Some of these travelling vendors were in very poor circumstances, only just managing to eke out their existence and it was not unusual in the early part of this century for some poor man or woman to call at the house with a petition which I believe was called a "brief" with the signature of either a parson or some other person in authority stating that the person named thereon has been unfortunate in losing his old horse which he depended upon and is not in a position to replace it and begging that you would contribute to enable him to buy another and so continue to earn a livelihood and support his wife and family. This custom was entirely within the law and was carried on for many years.

The Bruderhoff or "Society of Brothers"

THIS SOCIETY came and took up residence in Ashton Keynes about 1936. According to their own publication printed in 1940, a copy of which they sent to me in June

Members of the "Cotswold Bruderhoff" in typical national dress.

of that year the membership dwelling at Ashton Fields Farm and Oaksey Park Farm at that time consisted of three hundred and fifteen persons of as many as nine nationalities, including forty-eight British. The majority I would think were from Germany. There were forty-five families with one hundred and thirty children among them. They were people who for religious or political reasons had decided to break away from ordinary life. Some had already suffered imprisonment while some had escaped.

They first purchased Ashton Fields Farm, buildings and land, and set up as an entirely self-contained community with their own bakehouse, laundry, wood turning and carpenter's shops and printing works. They also tilled the land. As their numbers increased they purchased Oaksey Park Farm where they continued their activities. Before coming to this country their headquarters had been at Frankfurt, Germany. These had been confiscated by German agents and many of their members had been imprisoned. Their only hope was to flee the country which they did by many devious routes and methods, sometimes being assisted in their efforts by other Germans who were sympathetic towards them. Among them were a Dutch and a Swiss pastor.

Their system was not to pay wages but to share and share alike. The proceeds of any produce or articles sold went to a common fund so that all could participate. They did not claim to have cut themselves off from the world as their doors were always open, though they were all opposed to war. The only law which counted in their relationship was brotherly love but through contact with the state and the rest of mankind they realised that they were subject to the law of the land and were required to pay rates and taxes the same as anyone else.

They did however observe a certain discipline of their own without which they believed no Church could survive. Any conduct such as selfishness or un-brotherly behaviour would not be tolerated. Although a guilty person was not actually expelled by them it was reckoned that by his action he had expelled himself and therefore ceased to be a member or brother. This was a very sad but rare occurrence but the offender had the chance of "repentance," or turn away from his unbrotherly ways and once more become a member of the Bruderhoff.

Typical members of the "Cotswold Bruderhoff."

The Brotherhood was founded four centuries ago while their religion went back to the early Christian Church of nineteen hundred years ago.

I think that here I should mention that the money squeeze at that time was less tight than it is today and that they had no difficulty then in obtaining mortgages.

As it was necessary to guard against any chance of foreign agents entering the country the community was always subject to police inspection, especially after the outbreak of the 1939 war.

These people were without doubt industrious and enterprising. They had five motor vehicles on the road and at one time operated a retail milk round. When the war seemed to be coming close to their door they departed from the country. I remember attending their sale at Oaksey and buying up their large collection of milk bottles to keep in reserve in the event of their becoming unobtainable as I myself was delivering milk over a considerable area at the time.

I have heard that they went to Paraguay.

*   *   *   *

Between the Wars 1900 — 1914

AT the advent of the twentieth century and the close of the Boer War, it seemed to us who were children, attending school and reading our history books

110

that through the ages the country had been continually involved in War but that now War was a thing of the past and only to be read about in history books. But little did we know in our innocence what those who survived the next fifty years would have to endure. Rumours of war with Germany, story books recounting imaginary invasions were beginning to remind us that wars were not as we had thought a thing of the past, but that there were unmistakable signs that they were being prepared for by many countries on the continent of Europe.

It was decided to raise a Territorial Army for the defence of Britain, each county raising units of yeomanry, etc., training locally but with a week or two under canvas once a year.

In about 1911 big army manoeuvres were being carried out over the country, the Red Army versus the Blue. Up to then we had hardly seen a soldier in uniform, but as the armies moved about we had had what was really the first sight of what we were to see too much of in later years.

They were all enjoying the novelty of playing at soldiers. My wife — whose parents were farming at Buscot Wick — remembers how when they were camped nearby they would sing that old well-known song, "The Farmer's Boy" as they passed the farm. At Minety we had heard that they were expected through the village one evening. So we children ran up through the fields from the Moor to Minety Station bridge in time to see thousands of them on the march, their destination being Charlton Park where they intended to camp.

It had been a hot day. The old flint and stone roads were ground to powder and dust by the iron tyres of the guns and transport vehicles. The troops wore marching tunics unbuttoned at the neck, sweat and dust all over their faces and it seemed they were passing for hours. Infantry, cavalry and transport, all looking tired but still happy.

At about this time Colonel Pym was living at Braydon Hall and had raised a detachment of volunteers for the Wiltshire Yeomanry, a meeting having been held at the school for the purpose of recruiting. As an encouragement to the younger men, two middle-aged businessmen, Parish councillors, came forward and soon enough names had been submitted to make the project possible.

Now, at this time, the Yeomanry were mounted, a fact that these two prominent citizens were not yet aware of. There was a great difference between sitting as a reporter at the local Petty Sessions or operating a printing press and riding a horse of unknown quality. This was too much for one, who shall be nameless. He had already played his part in encouraging others. "No!" said he, "I've never mounted a horse yet and I certainly have no intention of doing so now. I refuse." Needless to say he never did. That's as far as that story goes.

Troopers in the Yeomanry were expected to ride a horse of their own, for which they were paid, if they had one, which many did who were farmers. One of the locals—whose father was a builder and wheelwright, undertaker and what-not— arrived for training in Braydon Park mounted on the old pony which they used for business purposes such as delivering coffins or loads of building materials. They were all drawn up in line when the Colonel gave the order "Mount!" Whether the old horse mistook the order history does not record, but as the troops turned to mount, the horse, tired of standing in the ranks had decided to lie down and take it easy. Believe it or not, this could well be true.

As we approached the second decade of the century the roll of drums was growing louder and in August 1914 the "balloon went up." We were at war. On that afternoon my family and friends were having a party at Charlton Pond. By making application to the then Lord Suffolk's agent you could have the use of one of the boats free of charge. While in the midst of our enjoyment the news was brought to us and I well remember the impact it had on everyone there. Everything seemed to come to a halt and there were wild speculations and rumours that the British and German fleets had had a collision in the North Sea. We went home with heavy hearts.

111

Kitchener was soon calling for his first hundred thousand men and they were answering the call. A large contingent was soon under training in Cirencester Park.

As a lad I happened to be in Cricklade Street, Cirencester, one day, standing on the steps outside Paternoster's the Chemist, when they came past singing as they marched, returning from a route march. Men of all descriptions, from all ranks of life, townsmen and countrymen, in straw hats, caps, trilbys and bowlers, some in good suits and some in tatters, but all seemed to be taking it as a matter of course.

As they sang their way back to Cecily Hill, the populace cheering them on, how little did they know what lay in store for them or what they would have to endure. How little did they know that in less than twelve months perhaps the majority of them would have paid the Supreme Sacrifice.

I for one am in favour of keeping up the tradition of "Remembrance Sunday" and only wish it could be brought more forcibly to the minds of this present generation. Living as so many do today under so much better conditions than their forefathers ever expected to or even dreamed of, let them remember, let it be taught in the schools to the children's children and let them never forget:—

"They died that we might live."

I think also that one might spare a thought for all the thousands of older men and women who have survived the holocaust of two wars, people whose lives, although spared, involved them in years of trial and ordeal and whose careers were changed or even ruined as a result, many of them enduring physical disability and suffering.

I had, however, read quite a lot about the various pioneer aviators, Bill Cody, Hubert Latham, the Wright brothers and many others including Lord Brabazon and M. Santos Dumont. The *Daily Mail* was sponsoring flights and putting up big prize money for such things as the first machine to fly a mile or complete a circuit, London to Manchester and so forth. Amongst it all a big prize was offered for the first heavier than air machine to make a flight over the Engilsh Channel. Our entrant, Latham, was frantically trying to beat the Frenchmen and was first away. Unfortunately he failed to qualify as he came down in the water after making an otherwise successful crossing. Before he could make a second attempt the Frenchman, M. Bleriot, had started off and made a good flight and landing.

Disposal of War Surplus

AT the time when World War I came to an end the world was just realising that flying had come to stay. There were many thousands of aircraft that were no longer needed and many thousands more in the process of being made. This in itself created quite a problem and much of this surplus accumulation was sold to the public either by auction or by tender.

At Steventon in Berkshire there seemed to be an unlimited supply of aeroplane wings, wooden struts, and beams tightened up by adjustable crossed wire bracings and covered with canvas and dope, camouflaged and complete with painted "roundels." These had come straight off the assembly line and had never even been fitted to a fuselage. What they had cost the country I would not hazard a guess, probably several hundred pounds each. They were actually "going for a song"— fighter wings four shillings each and "Handley Page" bomber wings at eight shillings each. My father happened to see some of them and ordered a truck load to be delivered to Minety Station and I was to fetch them home half a dozen or a dozen at a time. Imagine my surprise when I arrived home with an empty waggon. I don't think I had got out of the station yard before I had people clamouring for them at double the price we had paid for them, seeing the number of uses to which they could be put. Being very light to handle one man could carry a fighter wing easily, but the bomber wings being eighteen feet long and of stouter construction required a man at each end. This meant ordering another consignment and these also disappeared before I could get them home. They were used mostly for building sheds but they were also put to many other uses. Two Handley Page wings would cover quite a large area and it was possible to cut between the braces to any size required. Some were used for fencing and when the canvas became torn or rotten the frames were covered with galvanised iron. Eventually, most of them disappeared but even today after fifty years some bits and pieces are still to be found lying around.

As can be imagined there was a very large surplus of nearly every imaginable description such as Army huts, whole camp sites, and tools of every variety. Auction sales were held and camp sites bought up by contractors who dismantled them, advertising the timber, asbestos, galvanised iron, toilet fittings, etc. to be sold in small lots to the public. There was always a ready sale and as much of it was in sound condition it could be used in the erection of new buildings.

I remember going to the first Motor Cycle Show to be held after World War I, I think in 1919, travelling by motor cycle and sidecar, the first post-war model "Triumph" 4 h.p. Passing through Slough we saw hundreds if not thousands of disused motor vehicles varying from heavy lorries to cars and motor cycles in huge dumps covering acres and acres of ground. It was many years before they were finally disposed of. A large proportion of them were reconditioned and used again on the roads. Loads of this surplus war stock were brought to local sales besides the special sales and there was always a ready sale.

At the close of World War II there was a similar state of affairs, but during the years between the wars the armed forces had become much more highly mechanised in every respect. Also there was a very large number of American cars, Jeeps, lorries, etc. These were often collected on disused airfields or some other suitable site and sold by auction in lots of half a dozen or a dozen in a lot. So most of them were purhased by dealers and resold as there were not many who could afford to buy six when he only required one.

Then again as can well be imagined it was impossible for an eye to be kept on all this equipment, and of course the "bright boys" or "light fingered gentry" had usually paid a visit before the date of the sale so that a large number of the vehicles would be minus wheels, batteries, carburetters, instruments or in fact any removable parts so that if you wanted to buy one it may be necessary to purchase half a dozen to be sure you had all the parts to make one complete.

The Army Service vehicle then used by the American Forces was a four-wheel drive model named "Jeep" which was really descriptive of the initials "G.P." standing for General Purpose and it was actually the forerunner of the British version named the "Land Rover" which was very similar in design and appearance. The four-wheel drive gave them great advantages over the old conventional type of vehicle which had rear wheel drive only.

The Decoy Airfield

THE events of the '14–'18 war had proved beyond all doubt that air travel would be an absolute certainty in the future and that it would be vital for any country to maintain a strong Air Force. And so it was quite to be expected that Airfields would be established all over the country. This was especially the case in the southern parts of England, Wiltshire having a great number as also did Gloucestershire. On the Wiltshire border there was Kemble, nearby in Gloucestershire was Long Newnton, South Cerney, South Marston and Fairford, while on the Wiltshire side and all within a radius of a few miles there were airfields at Blake Hill (Leigh), Hullavington, Lyneham and Wroughton, also many others within a few miles in either direction.

In an attempt to divert a hostile attack on the airfields "Decoy Airfields" were built in order to attract raiders from their real objective. Through the network of Royal Observer Posts covering the country all airfields could be warned of any approaching enemy aircraft and so be prepared, in some cases by dispersing the machines on the ground and also by getting Fighters airborne ready to meet them and defend their base. On these occasions the "Decoy Airfield" was conspicuous by reason of having a few lights left on so as to appear from above as an actual airfield, thus deceiving the enemy into jettisoning his load of bombs clear of his objective.

Owing to the fact of Minety being so centrally situated and so surrounded by airfields the Air Ministry decided to construct a Decoy Airfield between Minety and Ashton Keynes, the site chosen being just south of the Swillbrook. The method adopted was to build a deep concrete shelter camouflaged with soil and greenery. Here a large engine was installed which in turn was coupled with a huge generator to create electric power. Wires were buried in all directions from Grange Farm, Swillbrook Farm and also two fields of the Moor Farm and Telling's Farm. The power house was manned by an R.A.F. Corporal and an airman who were in tele-phone communication with South Cerney R.A.F. Station. Their primary function was to attend to the engine and on receiving instructions from their headquarters to switch the lights on, also the floodlighting which illuminated the decoy runway. This runway ran across hedges and ditches and any large trees standing in the way were cut down leaving about four feet of the trunk standing. The ditches also were left open so that had any hostile aircraft attempted to land they would have undoubtedly come to grief.

Fortunately this never happened but quite a number of bombs were dropped in the area throughout the war. Night after night from 1940 onwards raiders were coming up from the coast of France mostly flying at great heights, but if they were flying at lower altitudes it was quite likely they were going to attack this vicinity. By far the most of the raids were carried out at night under cover of dark-ness, so that one got used to the droning overhead after retiring to bed.

It is hard for anyone who has not actually seen it to imagine the damage and havoc that a stick of bombs can make falling in the open fields. One bomb alone not only leaves a deep crater but also throws huge lumps of soil and timber that spread over many acres of land—land that the farmer is dependent on for his living. Much of this soil is rendered useless and impossible to pick up and the only way of getting the land back under cultivation again was to fill as many craters as we could with what soil we could collect leaving those in the less valuable places. Not only was this a great loss to the farmer and to the country but the jagged pieces of bomb-casing, splinters of metal etc. were a very considerable danger to cattle both by picking them up and by treading on them. Mowing the fields in summer also became dangerous through pieces of metal jamming the cutter bar of the mowing machine, breaking both cutting knives and sections. It was not unusual to finish a day's mowing with the toolbox on the outfit full of pieces of shrapnel which had been collected.

It would be impossible to praise too highly the men who actually did the spade-work on the construction of this particular Decoy Airfield. The firm of contractors responsible were Messrs. William Cowlin of Bristol, who brought the men every morning by road a distance of some forty miles, in a covered lorry. Practically every man belonged to some Civil Defence organisation in Bristol, either the Auxiliary Fire Service, the Red Cross or as Air Raid Wardens or in one or other of the many voluntary services. Bristol being almost continually under hostile air attack these men were often on duty all night, fire fighting, rescuing victims of bombed buildings often with hardly any rest at all before reporting for work again in the morning. Many of these men were veterans of World War I and long past the age for military service. Food rations were so meagre that when able I could not resist letting them have a few eggs off the ration. At that time eggs were so scarce that rationing only allowed one egg per person per week. There was no such thing as being able to make up with extra bacon or cheese as these also were rationed to a minimum of requirements.

As the Moor Farm House was situated within half a mile of the decoy the Air Ministry provided us with a protective blast wall and strengthened the roof and walls of one room with huge angle "H" section girders and concrete blocks. So at least we felt we had some element of security. But had we suffered a direct hit there could have been only one possible result—a heap of rubble. The fate of the occupants can well be imagined.

About the nearest escape we had was on Good Friday night, 1941 when a whole cargo of bombs was dropped just north of the house by about 200 yards or less. This load contained one or two thousand pounders and a time bomb which eventually exploded at twenty-three hours, but not until one of my sons and several other inquisitive persons had walked over it. However, the Police were soon on the scene and erected notices saying "UNEXPLODED BOMB" which soon had the desired effect, and answered the purpose, which goes without saying.

*   *   *   *

BEING born as I was at Flistridge or "Flustrygge" Farm and within the bounds of Bradon Forest, it is appropriate that I should recount the story of the people of Oaksey or "Woekeseye" and the "Abbot of Cruddewell" (Crudwell), Dr. Thomson in *Bradon Forest* from the Malmesbury Cartulary.

"It happened on the morrow of St. Michael, in the sixth year of King Edward that the Earl of Hereford being at the Manor of Wookeseye which is near the same wood of Flustrygge there came his people and the demesne hogs of the Earl and the hogs of his people of the town of Wookeseye into the aforesaid wood. Then came the Abbot's people of the town with great force and broke down the gates and forcibly took out the hogs and wounded the Abbot's people even to the death so that the Coroner was sent and all the country to look into this great affray. The hogs they forcibly drove back to the woods of Flustrygge and kept them there for fifteen days and upwards with great force of people so that no one of those who were with the Abbot dared to come near the wood. They forcibly kept them there until all the Mast was consumed."

The "Mast" referred to was probably acorns, as even in my day the pigs were allowed to roam the fields and would go from tree to tree and keep themselves for several weeks, not even returning at night while there were any acorns to be found.

The Manners and Maundrells

THE MANNERS FAMILY are old Wiltshire stock as also are the Maundrells. According to entries in the old family Bible of George Marler Maundrell (the sixth child of Joseph Maundrell who married Jane Marler on December 24th, 1816) the connection between the two families existed as far back at least as March 2nd, 1812 when a John Manners married Ann Maundrell, having ten children including Edward, my grandfather, born in 1820 who also married a Maundrell—Mary. They raised a family of three daughters and three sons, my father being the youngest son, born on April 28th, 1853. Although he was always delicate and had to lead an outdoor life on the farm, doing all his journeying either on horseback or driving a "trap" both in the heat of summer and snow, frost and east winds in winter, he lived to attain the age of seventy-seven years, all spent in the village of Minety.

The following extract from *Foxes Acts and Monuments* of 1556 is worthy of mention.

JOHN MAUNDRELL, THE MARTYR

John Maundrell was the son of a Wiltshire farmer, living at Rowde. When grown to a man he lived in the parish of Keevil in the same county, and, though unable to read, he always carried with him a copy of Tyndale's New Testament, and when he came into the company of any who could read, his Book was always ready to be produced. In the days of King Henry VIII, being accused of speaking against the Holy Water and Holy Creed, he was condemned to wear a white sheet and having a candle in his hand walk about the market of Devizes.

The Vicar of Keevil, going into his pulpit to pray for the souls in purgatory, John Maundrell said audibly "That was the Pope's pinfold" for which he was put into the stocks, and the next day sent to Salisbury and there imprisoned till his examination should take place.

At the last examination, accompanied by the Sheriff of the Shire, one, Master St. John and other opish priest in the Parish Church of Fi . . . (*print gone*) . . nger, he was asked "How did he believe?" He answered, "As a Christian . . viz: In God the Father, and in the Son, and in the Holy Ghost" . . (*print gone*. Possibly the Lord's Prayer, The Creed, the Holy Scripture from the first of Genesis to the last. *Print gone*).

Question: "Whether he did not believe the . . . Holy Sacrament of the Altar (as he termed it) after the words of Consecration spoken by the Priest at Mass, there remained no substance of Bread and Wine, but Christ's Body, Flesh and Blood, as He was born of the Virgin Mary?" He answered "No" saying that the "Popish Mass was abominable idolatory and injurious to the blood of Christ." He was asked if he believed that the Pope was the supreme Head of the Church and Christ the Vicar on earth. He answered "No" that the "Pope was anti-Christ and God's enemy." He was aksed whether souls in Purgatory were delivered by the Pope's pardons and the prayers of the Church? He answered that he "believed faithfully that the Blood of Christ had purged his sins, and the sins of them that were saved, unto the end of the World, so that he nothing feared the Pope's Purgatory nor esteemed his pardons."

He was asked if he believed that images were necessary in Churches and saints to be prayed unto and worshipped. He answered "No" adding that "wooden images were good to roast a shoulder of mutton, but evil in the Church whereby idolatory was committed."

For these answers he was condemned to be burnt to death, and the next day, the 24th of March, 1556, he was carried out of the common jail to a place between Salisbury and Wilton, where a post was set for him to be burnt at.

He knelt down, prayed secretly, and then being disclothed to his shirt, John Maundrell spake with a loud voice, "Not for all Salisbury" which was supposed to be an answer to the Sheriff who offered him the Queen's pardon if he would recant.

Thus this good man, with two companions, John Spicer and William Coberley, was burnt to death and his happy spirit has joined the glorious company of martyrs.

*   *   *   *

Wiltshire Moonrakers

NO BOOK OF WILTSHIRE STORIES would be complete unless it contained the legend of the "Wiltshire Moonrakers," the many versions of which differ widely. They all have, however, the same moral that not all Wiltshiremen are as simple as they may appear, and I think the following story is as good as any.

Although from time immemorial Wiltshire men have been expert cider makers and drinkers they were not averse to a taste of something more potent when the opportunity arose, and so, were apt to waylay the wagon trains that passed through on their way from the seaports to inland towns, and obtain from the drivers, possibly for a bribe, a keg or two of their cargo. On one occasion, having secured their booty, they were warned that some of the king's officers were in the vicinity. Fearing that they were in danger of being apprehended and of losing their ill-gotten gains they forthwith dumped the kegs in the nearest pond and returned to their homes with the intention of retrieving them on the night of the next full moon. This they did and arming themselves with hayrakes they proceeded to the pond by the light of the moon. They had just commenced dragging operations when suddenly a posse of the king's men arrived on the scene and started asking awkward questions, quite unaware of what lay at the bottom of the pond. The full moon was reflected on the water so one of the culprits answered, "We be trying to rake that there cheese out of the water"; whereupon the officers, thinking they were a lot of "looneys" or "country bumpkins" rode off and left them to it. Very soon the swag was recovered and they of course made off in the opposite direction—having completely outwitted the officers of the law.

CHAPTER SIX

A living from the land

ONE of the most significant changes to take place was in the reign of Elizabeth I in 1595 when it was decreed by the Privy Council that bows and arrows should no longer be issued as weapons of war but that firearms should be used henceforth. This was indeed one great step forward towards what we should perhaps call "modernisation." But the tremendous leap forward in the last few years, which incidentally have been largely during the reign of Elizabeth II is on a greater scale than ever before. I think it safe to say that the 20th century has seen more rapid changes in man's methods of travel by land, sea and air than has ever been known before besides vast strides in mechanisation in every sphere, in industry, warfare and not least in the field of agriculture.

Farming and Milk Production

UNTIL the nineteenth century nearly all field work was done by hand. Horses and oxen were used to draw the plough and harrows, haymaking being done almost entirely without mechanical aids. The grass was cut with a scythe held by two nibs on a long curved handle. As the worker moved forward he cut a swath about five feet wide. It was a good man who could mow an acre a day. The grass was tossed about with long-handled forks and hand-raked ready for "cocking up" when it was considered dry enough. The "haycocks" were then carried and built into "summer ricks" in the field, each of about half a waggon load. This method of "summer ricking" was to keep the hay secure from rain so that the farmer could get the greatest possible amount of hay while good weather lasted. The "summer ricks" were circular in shape, drawing to a point at the top usually held down by a "hayband" or "rope" made by drawing and twisting hay from the rick, until it is long enough to reach over the top and tuck in at each end.

In my boyhood days corn was threshed by hand with a "flail," two sticks joined by a leather thong. The corn was laid out on the ground and the grain beaten out by a man swinging the "flail" and threshing the straw (or whatever), which was then raked up. The grain that was left then had to be "winnowed" to extract dust, etc. from it and it was then gathered up into sacks. The first improvement on this method was the threshing drum, driven by a portable steam engine which seemed then to be the last word in luxury. This eventually gave

Crossley's Patent 5 Man Power "Otto" Gas Engine from an advertisement in 1885.

118

way to the combine harvester of today which cuts, threshes and bags, or blows it in bulk into an accompanying vehicle all in one operation. When these huge machines were first used they were horse-drawn with sometimes as many as eighteen or twenty horses in one team, now replaced of course by the farm tractor.

Modern methods have now transformed the entire operation of growing and harvesting cereals and roots on arable farms, while mechanisation for the dairy farmers producing milk, cheese and butter was also advancing.

Cheese and butter making are now almost entirely given over to the wholesale milk buyers who are able to convert the milk more economically in bulk than the farmers in individual units, but the production of milk by individual farmers is still very necessary. Milk production is now becoming the chief occupation of the dairy farmer besides the breeding of dairy and beef cattle.

In the early part of the century all the milk was produced by hand milking. A man who could milk six cows in full milk properly and cleanly in an hour was considered a fair milker. But no two cows were alike and no set time could be given. The man who recklessly sat under a cow and started operations in a manner that did not suit the cow very often found himself lying on his back on the ground, accompanied by his pail and the remains of any milk it had contained. In fact, as you got to know your cows you would know too, which ones were safe to sit under with milk already in the pail. The wise milker empties his pail between each cow. Some of the pails held four gallons but only with a quiet herd could you sometimes save time by milking more than one without emptying. Often when the cows got to know you and that you would handle them gently milking was quite a pleasant job and where large herds were kept a man might spend three or four hours of his working day sitting under cows. When things were going well the milker would be whistling or singing and the cow contentedly chewing the cud. What a contrast to the man working in a factory. At least the farm worker had peace and quiet and living as it were with the cattle he was never lonely. They could be quite good company and soon came to understand you as you understood them. Each cow was known by name. I once had one called "Sparkles" and I could wager anyone that if I went to the cowyard with my bucket and stool and sat in a certain place she would walk up and stand by me for me to milk her.

Alas, this atmosphere of peace and tranquility has now disappeared with the "milking machine" sweeping in on the wave of progress. With a mass of metal cups, rubber tubes, vacuum pumps and pulsators the cow is now approached in an entirely different manner, not always accepting the change which is inevitable.

First the cows were tied in rows in the milking shed and the unit of four cups and pail moved from cow to cow, the pail being attached to an overhead vacuum pipe. Then came "bail milking" where the cows are enticed with a feed of cattle cake a few at a time into a smaller shed, washed, milked and released when finished through a sliding door, not returning to the yard but passing forward as another batch is let in from the rear and so on until the whole herd has been milked. Pails are still used in many cases but the "parlour" method is now becoming into favour where the milk is carried by pipes directly to the churn or bulk container. Naturally these methods result in higher quality and cleaner milk.

As all milk today has to pass a very stringent test for bacteria, butter fat content and keeping quality, correct cleansing of all equipment and washing of the cows has to be observed. The unscrupulous producer would have his milk returned from the depot and could even lose his "milk producer" licence.

* * * *

Wilts. and Somerset Farmers in Voluntary Liquidation

IT must have been soon after World War I that we first became involved with a firm of Milk Wholesalers, Milk Contractors and Dealers in Corn, Seeds,

Staddle Stones. These stones, many of which may be seen decorating gardens and driveways were not originally intended for this purpose. Before the use of the Combine Harvester, when corn was stacked in sheaves prior to the grain being threshed out, it would become infested with rats which devoured the grain causing considerable loss to the farmer and to the country. It was found that by erecting the stacks on staddle stones with rails connecting them, the rats were unable to reach the grain as they could not climb the stones. Staddle Stones were also used under granaries in many places.

Feedingstuffs, Fertilisers and Coals. The first reference I have is dated February 21st, 1920 headed "The Wiltshire Farmers Limited." This firm was later known as "Wilts and Somerset Farmers Limited" and had no connection with the present firm "Wiltshire Farmers Limited."

Now this firm was offering slightly better prices for milk than were being offered by other companies and this naturally attracted the interest of many local farmers. There was one condition to be complied with by the unfortunate farmer who succumbed to this enticing offer. It was that he would be required to become a shareholder, the shares being at the equivalent of so much of share capital per head for each of his dairy cows. A certain percentage could be paid in cash by the farmer, the balance being deductable from the monthly milk cheque at the rate of sixpence per gallon of milk until the total amount of share capital had been paid.

It came as a bombshell and almost meant ruination to many local farmers when in 1922 the firm became insolvent. On February 15th a meeting of creditors was called, to be held in the Neeld Hall, Chippenham, when the firm finally went into liquidation and Sir Gilbert Garnsey was appointed Official Receiver.

I myself attended this meeting journeying to Chippenham on my motor cycle. Eventually after many meetings and much discussion a letter was circulated on May 2nd, 1923, acknowledging receipt of claims and setting forth the figures. The amount owing to my father was fifty-five pounds, seven shillings and nine-pence, which after various adjustments and contra accounts for goods and feeding stuffs supplied was reduced to thirty-two pounds, nine shillings and twopence.

But the axe was to fall again yet heavier. To be deducted from this amount was the balance of the uncalled capital so that from what I can understand of the communication dated January 28th, 1925, instead of receiving a small cheque which would have been better than "no bread," my father was actually in debt to the Company to the tune of one pound, seventeen shillings and ninepence. As can be imagined in some cases this was the cause of much hardship, particularly as it came at a time of depression in the milk producing industry.

N.B. I have since found a communication from Messrs. Price, Waterhouse & Co. stating that a dividend of 5/- in the pound was being paid and enclosing a cheque for £7-10-0d. which was, as can well be imagined, most acceptable.

*   *   *   *

Having had a life's experience of farming in North Wiltshire, mostly dairy farming, this being clay subsoil and not particularly adaptable for growing cereal crops, many other changes come to my mind.

During the war of 1939-45 the War Agricultural Committee took over certain farms or parts of farms where they thought the occupiers were not producing as much as the land was capable of. Much of this land they ploughed, cultivated and planted with wheat or barley. Owing to the unpredictable weather that farmers are always at the mercy of, these crops were never harvested. I have seen two of their combine harvesters bogged down in a twenty acre field where they had to remain until such time as they could be moved by crawler tractors and the crops left for the birds or to rot on the ground. It has been proved by experience over the last thirty or forty years that some old pasture that has deteriorated to not much more than weeds and flowers with a good undergrowth of moss, producing poor grazing and poor quality hay, can be vastly improved by ploughing and reseeding, and made to produce enough to satisfy the countrywide appeal of the Government, which, to quote the wartime slogan was, "To make two blades of grass grow where one grew before," thus enabling the land to carry more cattle per acre and also to produce more hay.

It is a sad thing to have to say, but the unfortunate fact is that the main plank in the platforms of the politicians is, more or less, "cheap food for the workers," and the agriculturist—being the minority voter—is sacrificed to get the support of the industrial workers. Agriculture was the poor relation until the country became involved in war. Then when imports were being cut off or sunk to the bottom of the sea it was realised too late that it had been allowed to fall into decay.

There are many hazards which affect the price of agricultural products as against industrial manufacturers. The big problem the farmer has to battle with all the year round is the weather. Wet, dry, winds and frost, all can cause major calamities. I have known crops of all descriptions flattened and ruined by heavy rain and wind, fruit blossom cut off by frost, corn unable to be carried, cattle starving for grass and water and good fruit crops stripped from the trees by freak hailstorms with hailstones as big as walnuts or eggs also smashing greenhouses. I have seen crops of hay washed away by floods before it could be picked up or having to rot on the ground on account of continual rain. I have seen stocks of wheat standing in the fields, green at the tops where the grain has fertilised and started to grow out even before it had been threshed. All this of course means a tragic loss to the farmer who, if he is a tenant farmer, still has to pay the same rent, but is equally disastrous for the owner-occupier.

Sometimes a herd of cattle is struck by "foot and mouth disease." Up to the present time the only remedy is to slaughter every animal. A good productive herd which has taken the farmer many years to build up can be written off in a flash. Admittedly there is some compensation from the Ministry of Agriculture but this is small comfort in the face of loss of income and a lifetime's work.

Added to this, the industrial manufacturer can fix the price of his products to show a definite profit based on production costs whereas the farmer has to sell his produce at prices fixed by the Ministry of Agriculture. If production costs rise by such items as higher cost of labour, feeding stuffs etc., the farmer has to submit evidence to the Ministry (who are already aware of the fact that costs have risen) and to substantiate their claim for better prices. If the farmers can prove that the extra burden on them is for example in the region of £10,000,000 a year the government may allow a price increase of half that amount and tell the farmers they must recover the remainder by using more economical methods of production. Everywhere you hear the cry of the drift of labour from the land to the towns. This is inevitable with the introduction of more and better machines and larger farming units. This and enormous imports are the only answer if the country is to be fed.

The following figures will give some idea of fluctuations in prices over the years.

In 1896 five fat steers made £15 each. This meant a loss to the dealer so the farmer gave him £1 back on the deal. Fat sheep fetched 6d. to 8d. per pound and cheese 4d. and 5d.

In 1900 three cows sold for £26, wheat at 30/- per quarter; bacon 7/6 per score (20lbs.); charge for threshing was 2/4d. per day.

Looking through the account books of an uncle of mine who was a registered farrier and shoeing smith I quote some of the charges for work done in 1905-7:

To shoe a horse all round. Shoes inclusive, about 1ft. iron per shoe, per set of shoes fitted	2/8d.
One remove	4d.
Frost nailing all round	9d.
1 shut link	1d.
Handle to hayfork	1/-
Hang and grind scythe	6d.
Grind hook	3d.
Cutting, shutting (welding) and bonding cart wheel, including approximately 12ft. of iron tyre (about 3in. x ½in.)	4/-
For bonding a barrow wheel	1/-

Out of this he had to pay a man's wages and buy faggots of wood to heat up the tyres before fitting and coal for the forge.

The method used to bond a wooden cart wheel with an iron tyre was to lay the strip of iron on the ground, stand the wheel on one end and clamp it on. Next, two men rolled the wheel along until the iron encircled it marking it with chalk and then a chisel at the required length. The two ends were then heated in the forge and welded together by two men striking with heavy hammers. The tyre was then laid on a bonfire of faggot wood and well heated all round. The wheel itself in the meantime had been laid on a circular heavy iron plate and screwed down in the centre. The tyre was then taken from the fire, laid over the wheel, tapped down flush all round, then cold water was applied from watering cans as quickly as possible so that the fellows of the wheel were not burnt. As the tyre cooled down the metal contracted, so making a tight fit. This tyre would last for many years, and all this for the sum of four shillings. It is scarcely believable.

Prior to the setting up of the Milk Marketing Board in 1933 farming was at a very low ebb. In the dairying districts most farmers had switched from butter and cheese-making to wholesale milk selling. With the coming of the railway there came a demand for milk for liquid consumption which enveloped Wiltshire. This demand had been gradually developing for several years. Milk at first was sold wholesale by a measure not used today, *viz.* the "barn gallon" which consisted of two imperial gallons and one pint, or seventeen pints. The milk churn in use was made to hold eight "barn gallons" or seventeen imperial gallons of eight pints. At one time, I recollect the price per "barn gallon" varied around a shilling delivered to London by rail.

The train carrying this milk left the local railway station—Minety and Ashton Keynes—at 8-10 a.m. and woe betide the man who arrived too late. On a frosty morning the beat of horses' hooves could be heard for miles converging from every direction as they were driven mercilessly to catch the milk train There was great competition among the farmers as to who could drive the best or the fastest turnout. I can remember to this day seeing some of the horses standing in the station yard with sweat streaming from their bellies while the drivers were frantically looking for empty milk churns to take back. This was always a problem, making sure of enough empties for the next evening and morning's milking. Each farmer had his name punched on a brass plate on the churn lids which were detachable, and there was always a general "melee" and grabbing of churns and interchanging of lids. But in spite of it all everyone was happy and it was not often that they came to blows. After the matter of the churns was settled the farmers always enjoyed a few minutes' chat with each other about the weather, the crops or the state of the market.

It is no exaggeration to say that at one time there were no less than sixty vehicles at this station alone with loads of milk for the London train and we sadly missed the excitement when the Combines not content with the profit they made, decided they must also be collectors of milk, setting up local depots and picking the milk up from the farms themselves. Their charge for this plus an additional charge for handling at the depot, which they termed "Standard Freight Deduction," was considerably higher than that of the railways which was just over one penny per gallon. Also, it was not long before they conceived the idea of "combining" which meant that they all agreed to offer the same price so that the farmers had to accept this instead of being able to bargain for a better one. These combines also introduced a clause into their contract, which was for twelve months' supply of milk at a time, which stated that if at any time milk sent in by the producers exceeded the demand for liquid milk consumption, this over-plus milk could be paid for at what they described as "manufacturing price." Naturally, in the spring when cows were turned out to grass the milk yield rose and I have known times when 50% of milk produced in May and June has been paid for at this "manufacturing price" which was just 4d. per imperial gallon. Nothing much could be done about it. The National Farmers' Union seemed nervous of taking any drastic action.

When matters seemed at their lowest ebb and I was a member of the Malmesbury Branch of the Union I felt so strongly about it that I refused to sign my contract, offering to burn it in the Market Place. But without the support of the Union, everyone was afraid so I stood out alone and did not sign, deciding to go back to butter making and pig keeping. This was, of course, a long-term policy.

Buying a stock of gilts meant that I had to wait twelve months for any return on my outlay, a pig having to be six months of age before she could be used for breeding purposes with a further gestation period of sixteen weeks. The young piglets then have to be kept with the sow for ten weeks. This nearly brought a financial disaster as farming had slumped to such an extent that I actually sold pigs in Cricklade Market at 4/6d. per head—one litter I actually sold at 2/6d. per head—and slightly better pigs at Wootton Bassett for 7/6d.

Having to try to keep afloat minus a milk cheque and with butter making only about 1/- per pound I soon found myself at the mercy of the milk combines again. However, at that time the "Accredited Milk Scheme" came into operation which meant that milk produced under especially hygienic conditions and which passed a rigid test for low bacteriological count or absence of, merited an extra 1¼d. per gallon. So I wrote to the Milk Department of the Wiltshire County Council to ask them to send their Inspector to draw up a list of the necessary modifications and improvements I should be required to carry out in order to produce this accredited milk. In due course I was favoured with a visit from the Agricultural Officer, who, I believe was at that time Mr. Hugh McLees.

All walls with which the cows came into contact had to be rendered with impervious material, usually cement or flat galvanised iron sheets to a height of four feet, all effluent to be carried away via inspection traps and septic tanks, also the dairy had to be rendered to a height of four feet and the roof sealed in. All dairy utensils would have to be steam sterilised and cows lying in the stalls in the winter months—as all milking cows are—had to be machine clipped around the hind quarters and udder.

This was a formidable undertaking but there seemed no escape. So I set to with a will, single handed except for my wife and had the job ready for inspection by the local authorities in three months. My premises passed the test and my dairy was declared suitable for the production of accredited milk. This seemed a a great achievement, but all this for a paltry 1¼d. a gallon more for my milk. To rub salt into the wounds, when this hygienically produced milk arrived at the local depot it was tipped wholesale into the tanks with ungraded milk which to my mind defeated the efforts of all the trouble we had been put to.

What seemed to be the turning point of my farming career was when I took over a small retail milk round in the thirties. The retail price of milk was then 3d. per pint or 2/- per gallon. The Milk Marketing Board had come into operation and I was required to register as a producer retailer and as I was an accredited producer I was asked by the local authorities if I would undertake to supply the local schools, there being two schools at Minety. I also agreed to supply the Leigh and Ashton Keynes schools. All this school milk had to be delivered in ⅓-pint bottles which meant a great deal of work for my wife and daughter. Under the school milk scheme, parents were asked to pay 1d. per bottle except in special cases where it was free. The balance I had to claim from the County Council.

During this time World War II started to disrupt everything. Milk, as well as petrol, went on ration, also feeding stuffs for cattle which could only be claimed according to your returns of milk production. I was therefore obliged, much against my will, to refuse my customers more than their ration, although they would have paid anything to get it. My ration of food for the cattle was based on the number of registered customers on my returns so that it would have been impossible to obtain extra cattle food to cover it. Had it not been for this I am sure I would have felt tempted to take the risk in many instances where in my opinion people were getting insufficient milk for their needs. The allowance of milk was limited to half a pint per head per day and one egg per week. I have had to walk many miles to deliver this half-pint of milk and one egg, some houses with a single occupant being off the road. But everyone had to be fed, regardless of whether there was any profit in it.

T.T. Milk Production

As we advanced into the twentieth century and the population of the country was vastly increasing, so the health of the public in general was becoming a greater problem which had to be grappled with by the medical profession, the Ministry of Health and the Ministry of Agriculture. As it was generally believed that milk, being a staple diet, could spread disease unless produced hygienically and from healthy cows, the ministries concerned launched the "Accredited Milk" scheme and enforced a "Milk and Dairies" order which required that all milk sold must be produced on registered premises and under hygienic conditions. Attention now had to be turned to the health of the animals.

For many years a disease — Bovine Tuberculosis — had been rife among milking herds. It was found that germs were present in milk from an infected cow and could be a health risk to consumers, especially to those with a low resistance. So a scheme for the eradication of this disease was introduced so that a tuberculin tested grade of milk could be produced. Every cow in the herd was given a blood test by an approved veterinary surgeon and any "reactors" were weeded out.

Having held an "accredited milk" producer's licence since 1937, a fact of which I had felt rather proud, I was beginning to feel by 1951 that I was lagging behind and so I decided to have my herd tuberculin tested privately by my own veterinary surgeon, Mr. L. Constance of Malmesbury. This test, to my great disappointment showed at least fifty per cent to be reactors, thus creating a very big problem. "No time like the present" was always a maxim of mine. After a long discussion with my "vet" I decided to do as he suggested and to sell every animal on the farm regardless. "Reactors" had not been condemned as being unfit for human consumption and could be sold in the open market. I would then keep the land free from cattle of any description for at least three months during which time I could knock out all wood partitions or any wooden structures with which the cows had been in contact, thoroughly disinfect the premises and erect new tubular cow ties and water bowls, then having got the house in order replace the herd with tuberculin tested cattle from an area which was already scheduled as clean and one hundred per cent eradicated of the disease.

I sold the whole of the herd in one lot to a dealer friend of mine, Mr. Templar Greenaway of Cirencester, and then consulted Mr. Hew Carruthers who at the time was farming at Murcott Farm, Crudwell, and running a herd of tuberculin tested Ayrshires, a breed known to give a high yield and producing milk of a high butter fat content. He gave me the name of his agent in Scotland who lived in Dumfries which was an "eradicated" area.

I met him at Swindon market and arranged with him, as he knew the area and was familiar with the breeders and markets while I was not, for a start, to purchase and collect for my inspection fourteen first-calf heifers, already calved and tried on the milking machine. The calves to be sold away as they could not be expected to survive a journey of four hundred miles in a cattle lorry. I agreed to pay him £65 each regardless of what they had cost him and I also gave him a bonus of £5 to select what he thought were likely to turn out as good milkers.

Having contacted Messrs. Austin Clarke & Sons to be ready with their largest cattle truck I gave them a ring directly I got the wire from Scotland. It arrived at the Moor Farm at 6 p.m. one evening and we set out on the 400 miles round trip. My son John accompanied me and Richard Clarke was at the wheel. We somehow collected a stowaway, who no doubt needing a cheap trip to Scotland, travelled in the calf department above the driving cab. As is usually the case he was soon discovered, but Mr. Clarke, being a humane sort of fellow, allowed him to remain. With a twelve-hour journey through the night my son, being in need of sleep, soon joined him there.

We did not lose much time except for refreshment and after climbing the notorious "Shap Fell" we all had a short sleep. Then after passing through Gretna Green as dawn was breaking we arrived at our destination at 6 a.m.

To cut a long story short, we met our agent and with his help selected our quota. The lady of the house, after giving us a good meal, allowed us to sleep on comfortable beds upstairs until about 5 p.m. We then loaded up the cattle and headed south. It was necessary to make frequent stops to make sure that none of them was down or being trampled on and eventually at exactly six o'clock on the morning of the third day we arrived safely back at the Moor Farm.

Lest anyone should jump to conclusions, this was not the end. After unloading the cattle we had to round them up and tie them in a strange pen and get the milking machine into action as these heifers were all freshly calved and in the flush of milk. They had not been milked since early afternoon of the previous day and milk was streaming out of them. We ourselves were nearly played out and it was mid-day before we had got them all foddered and milked. We just fell on our beds and slept, but not for long for the simple reason that they all had to be milked yet again in the afternoon.

I never felt safe in buying tuberculin tested cattle from a local market where they could possibly come into contact with untested animals. So I made up my herd to about twenty-five by buying direct from Mr. Carruthers and Mr. Wardle Smith of Field Farm, Minety, and then built up my herd to about forty by rearing my own calves. From the time I started my herd of tuberculin tested cattle, although they had to be tested every twelve months, I never once had a single reactor. I would like to mention the fact that untested cows were much cheaper on the market and that I had to sell forty of these to pay for twenty tuberculin tested.

Agricultural Wages, etc.

AGRICULTURAL wages have never been high as everyone knows and until land started being enclosed everyone grew their own food on their Common Allotment. But when the Enclosure Acts made it compulsory for the Commoner to enclose his land this was beyond the means of many, either through bad husbandry or through reasons beyond their control. These therefore were obliged to sell their portion of land to another and thus it was that there was the employer and the employed. Also, when the time came that each parish was made responsible for the upkeep of its own highways local employment became available for many.

Some of the figures taken from the "Surveyor of the Highways" account book for the parish of the Leigh commencing in the year 1837 make very interesting reading. Wages paid to men employed on this work was, for many years, 1/2d. per day or 7/- per week. A man working three days received 3/6d.

These rates varied slightly from time to time. The rate of pay for hauling flints was 3/6d. to 3/9d. per yard (approximately 25 cwt.). These flints were dug locally.

For the relief of the poor there was a "Poor Rate" of 4d. in the pound.

In the year 1837 there was "Composition Rate" which raised the sum of £11-9-0d. and it would appear that this did not seem sufficient. For in the entry for 1848-9 there is a "Poor Rate" of 4d. which raised £32-7-1d. As evidence of the rising cost of living in those days, by 1850 the rate had risen to 6d. in the pound, bringing in the sum of £42-16-4d. This, however, appears to have proved too harsh a treatment for in the year 1851 the rate was reduced to 3d. This reduction could possibly have been due to a higher rent being paid for "Poor's Platt" which was distributed annually for the relief of the poor and varied from about £28 to £50 per annum, although for some unknown reason in the year 1866 it amounted to £77-10-0d. and the payments made to those participating rose from £1 to an average of over £2 each. Five families who had more children received as much as £3. This was very rare. This "Poor's Platt" was let annually by auction at Cricklade.

A typical entry in the account book of the "Leigh Poor's Platt" for 1840 is as follows:—

Received from Mr. Edw'd Francome a year's rent for Poor Platt. Due Lady Day, 1840	£54	0	0
Received the Balance of last year's Accounts and brought from the old book	£6	3	1
	£60	3	1

Disbursements made by John Brain to Lady Day 1840:

A year's salary due to John Brain for keeping the accounts of the Platt, March 25th	10 0
March 25th, 1840. Paid the expenses of the letting of the Platt	5 0
March 26th. Paid the Cryer for crying the letting of the Platt, etc.	2 0
Paid John Taylor for destroying the moles in the do.	2 6
Paid for two books	5 3

Then follows a list of those receiving the proceeds.

There have been many bequests in the past for the benefit of the poor, many of which still hold good, are in the hands of the Charity Commissioners and are distributed annually in kind, such as coal, etc., or otherwise in money. The local Parish Councils usually submit the names of those eligible. Some even extend to helping apprentices by giving a grant towards cost of tools, etc.

Since the end of the nineteenth century however, agricultural wages have been steadily improving. In 1906-7 the labourer was paid 12/- per week on a dairy farm and 15/- during the haymaking season, the rate of overtime varying, but usually about 4d. per hour.

By the thirties it had risen to about £1-10-0d. and by 1941 the weekly wage was £2-8-0d. By 1943 it was £3 minimum, by 1962 it had leapt to around £7, with overtime, and by 1965, including overtime, to about £14. In 1970 the latest figures of the Agricultural Wages Board stipulate that the minimum rate for a man aged 20 or over shall be as from February, £13-3-0d. basic, which on a dairy farm where often twelve hours have to be paid for at overtime rates, now 9/2 per hour, the total comes to £18-13-0d.

This is not a high wage in comparison with other industries but when it is borne in mind that the wholesale price of milk has been practically stationary for ten years some idea can be gained of the unequal struggle the British farmer is waging. It is a great pity there is no William Cobbett today to air his views. They would scorch the paper they were written on.

CHAPTER SEVEN

Diversions

Entertainment

THE present generation may wonder how village folk spent their time before the days of cars, buses, radio, television, etc. Most people had a pig in the sty and some allotment to cultivate and it was customary after tea on light evenings to walk to the allotments with some kind of gardening tool over their shoulder, attend to their alloted piece for an hour or so, then get together for a gossip or a half pint at the local. There was usually an open space on the village green or other place where they could play cricket or whatever field sport was in favour at the time. Also throughout the summer months there were always the Annual Horse and Flower Shows being held in the surrounding villages.

Oaksey Races

An event which was looked forward to with great excitement was "Oaksey Races" organised annually by the Vale of White Horse Hunt. This drew more traffic to the area than anything either before or since. I remember as a child attending the Silver Street school, the pupils sitting on the gates and stiles and lining the bank opposite to the school to watch an almost endless procession of horses and vehicles. There was no such thing as horseboxes then. There were grooms with saddle horses, some to run in the races, single horse traps and gigs with all seats filled to capacity, wagonettes drawn by pairs, carriages and pairs, four-in-hand, with harness and brasses polished up for the occasion, high-stepping hacks and the occasional half bred or big boned farmer's horse with market trap or dog-cart. A motley procession the memory of which will never be blotted out.

The races were held at Oaksey Park, several of the surrounding Hunts taking part. The races and the horses there were of a high standard. All local farmers received from the Hunt Secretary two luncheon tickets, complimentary. I have a faint recollection of the bread and cheese, pickled onions and beer that was served at long tables in the large marquees between races. I believe that after the Great War Oaksey Races were discontinued but the Hunt ran them at Swatnage, Preston (Siddington) and Blunsdon. I did not attend for a great number of times but one incident comes to my mind when there was a fatal accident during one of the races, and I was standing only a few yards away. Capt. Faber was among the leaders when his horse made a mistake and both came to the ground. He had no chance of getting clear of the rest of the field, which seemed bunched up, and were unable to avoid landing right on him.

These "Point to Point" Races are still held to this day as a traditional part of the English way of life. Fortunately such accidents as this are very few. In fact I have not heard of a single one during a race in this neighbourhood since.

This does not mean in any way that there were no accidents on the roads in those days. In fact there were almost as many as there are today, caused by horses and horse drawn vehicles. Many horses were very dangerous kickers. In the hunting field these were identified by having a red ribbon tied round the dock, i.e. high up on the tail. Many were the accidents and injuries caused by a kick from a horse. A cousin of mine was killed in this way. Riders were thrown, horses bolted

Oaksey Race Day—in the old days.

with their conveyances and it was no unusual sight to see a horse wildly careering down the road, one wheel on the grass verge where there were often heaps of stones put there for road mending. Sometimes a trap would overturn and catapult its occupants on to the road. A story goes of a man who was given a lift by his neighbour. The horse bolted and the wheel of the trap was bouncing over the stone heaps. Getting scared he said to the driver "I'd give something to be out of this," whereon the reassuring reply he got was "Don't worry. Thee'l be out on't for nought in a minute."

I shall never be able to forget the most miraculous of the many escapes from death that I have had during my lifetime. It was a dark, wet, and rough night. As was our usual habit, my neighbour and I were walking together to the Sunday evening Service where we sang in the Church Choir. Having had cattle work and milking to do we were rather short of time and so took a short cut across the fields. As the grass was sodden and wet we decided to get on to the railway line at the Lower Moor and walk as far as the level crossing near Brandier's Farm and complete the journey by road. We knew we were trespassing and liable to a fine of forty shillings but the risk was worth it. We made it a rule to walk facing oncoming trains which should be seen at a reasonable distance as they carried a small oil lamp on the front of the engine.

Owing to the gale blowing and the wind whistling over the embankment we could hear nothing but on seeing a light approaching we immediately stepped over on to the down line until the train had passed. The train made noise enough as it passed and all seemed well until we seemed to sense that the noise was getting louder instead of dying away. Glancing round we saw to our horror that there right on our heels was another train nearly on top of us. We threw ourselves out of the way, tripped over the signal cables and went sprawling without a moment to spare. The choir were very near to being one tenor and one bass short that night.

Rook Shooting

IN the early part of this century the country was much more densely timbered than it is today with mostly oak, elm and a fair amount of ash. The hedgerow trees

129

were planted when the Enclosure Acts were passed and I remember how my hair used to tingle and stand on end on a dark night when I might have been walking home from the Social Club at the school, or out on some similar jaunt, when suddenly in a tree, overhead there would be a rustling sound and an owl would give an eerie "Hoot." If you were alone this made your heart beat a bit faster but as one grew older even stray cattle or horses became a customary hazard.

At that time one of the most common birds to be be seen in the countryside was the Rook. In the Spring they would gather where the trees were thickest and start nesting, sometimes fifty or more, perhaps a hundred, forming what was known as a Rookery. These birds were a menace on the corn land and every year when the young were ready to fly the local farmers passed the word around, and on an agreed evening every man who could get hold of a gun, single or double barrelled, breach or muzzle loaded, let fly at them with devastating effect. As a rule the farmers were experienced with the gun and good shots and most of the other members of the party were either well practiced in the art of poaching or else in the habit of carrying a gun when taking a stroll in the fields. It is open to doubt as to how many of them ever took out a gun licence which, it was said was not necessary if the weapon were only used for the destruction of vermin. I remember once when I was a lad an act was passed that all firearms that were rifled in the barrel had to be registered with the police. It happened one day when a "Swine Fever" order had been imposed, there being an outbreak at the time, and it was forbidden for any pigs to be moved off the premises. As usual a Police Officer called at the farm to notify us of this and while there he noticed a rifle standing by the back door. He picked it up, peered down the barrel and asked my brother if he had registered it. As he had not done so the officer said he would call again with an application form for registration to be filled in. One of the questions was "For what purpose is this firearm required?" The saying goes "Always ask a policeman" so my brother asked him how he should answer, to which the officer replied "Oh, just put 'Because it is in my possession'." No doubt a drop of rough cider may have helped matters. He was a very pleasant and likeable fellow and ever ready to smooth things over when possible.

*　　*　　*　　*

V.W.H. Hunt

WILTSHIRE, situated as it is in the southern part of the country has always played its part. Ever since the landing of the Romans under Julius Caesar, in the progress or evolution of this country, this county has been involved in perhaps more fighting than any other. Much evidence of this is to be found in the numerous Barrows and remains of earth works seen almost everywhere. In ancient times when England consisted of more than one Monarchy, Wiltshire was the predominant and main centre of the Kingdom of Wessex, and has all through the ages been the favourite hunting ground of the Monarch, including as it did the Braydon Forest which at one time was said to cover more than fifteen thousand acres.

Lodges were built in many places where royal parties could be accommodated with their followers and servants. Many of these still exist or the sites are known. To name but a few, there is Penn's Lodge, (Wiltshire being claimed as the birth-place of William Penn who gave his name to Pennsylvania), Gryphon Lodge, White Lodge, Red Lodge and also one on the Common Fields known as the Lodge Hills. On Braydon Hall estate there is a house still known as "The Lodge" although this one has evidently been rebuilt in fairly recent years.

Gloucestershire was also good hunting ground, Cirencester being the seat of the Earls Bathurst. Cirencester Park, with woods of ten miles radius and drives, provided excellent shooting and hunting. Consequently the Manners family have always been known to have kept some good horses and for very many years were regular riders to hounds with the V.W.H. (Bathurst) or more often the V.W.H. (Cricklade). At least four generations have carried on the tradition. In this way one was able to assess the horse's performance or its prospects of making a good steeplechaser.

Besides entering horses in the local Hunt Point to Point, as they were called, there have been occasions when they were tempted to go for bigger stakes, not always in vain. In the year 1946, Ernest Manners entered his horse "Prattler" at Cheltenham and won the National Hunt Steeplechase. This horse was well placed in the Grand National at Aintree the same year, when unfortunately like many others it was unlucky enough to fall. However, the year 1968 was a red letter year in more ways than one, for the Aintree classic was won by Red Alligator owned by John Manners and ridden by Brian Fletcher.

From owning good horses to the other extreme; it was surprising the trouble many would take, myself included, to get hold of a mount whenever there was a meet of the local foxhounds within a reasonable distance. There is no disgrace in riding upon an ass, and when my Grandmother Manners, who died in 1906, gave us as children a young donkey, I with nothing else to ride (as the fashion of keeping ponies for the very young was not as popular as it is today, for the simple reason that small farmers were not always sufficient in funds to go to this expense) took many a day off from school to follow the Hunt riding the donkey. He was very "hard on the mouth" and had such a tremendously thick coat and skin that all my efforts with a stick had no effect whatsoever if he decided to go in a particular direction and usually when we came to a fence I would have to dismount, get behind him and push him through the hedge with my shoulder. I remember on one occasion when we were drawing the "Fox-Cover" on the Minety House estate my old "moke" had been determined to trot up amongst the hounds. The Master and Whips were all shouting at me, but to no avail. I think I turned rather red in the face, the situation being completely out of control.

This effort of mine was written about 1907 when I was ten years of age.

It was at the time I rode a donkey to hounds. There may be some who can still remember this unusual sight, and the incident of the badgers.

MY BEST RIDE

T'was a bright winter's morning
    And not very sleek
When Earl Bathurst's hounds
    At the "Old Inn" did meet.

I saddled my "Nirrup"
    And put on my spurs
Sprang into the stirrup
    And patted his ears.

We went off to Hankerton
    And drew at ten sharp
Then moved off to Charlton
    And 'lost' in the Park.

They scented a badger
    And soon ran it to ground
We made him a deader in
    A couple of rounds.

My steed was nigh winded
    Time was slipping along.
I went back to my kindred
    And soon got back home.

131

More on Hunting

I have the diary for 1876 kept by my father with an entry "Went Hunting with His Royal Highness the Prince of Wales. The meet was at Eastcourt House. Father, Herbert, Edward and I went. I rode Little Polly." His Royal Highness, afterwards King Edward VII, was staying at Cirencester. H.R.H. The Prince of Wales stayed at Cecily Hill with the Earl and Countess of Shannon for three days' hunting. Two with the V.W.H. and one with the Cotswold.

The story goes that the Member of Parliament for Malmesbury at the time, Mr. Walter Powell, who also hunted with the Bathurst Pack had laid on a lavish lunch and engaged extra staff to entertain the royal party previous to the hunt moving off. Some say that there were political moves behind it and some that His Royal Highness was anxious to get mounted and away, but the fact remains that after all Powell's preparations and expense they ignored the invitation and moved off immediately.

This was a very great disappointment for Mr. Powell as he had made elaborate arrangements besides laying on a lavish spread. When the hunting party moved off Mr. Powell threw the doors of the house open to all the local inhabitants who had gathered to see the royal party and invited them to come in and enjoy the feast, this no doubt giving him some consolation.

However, he took it very much to heart and soon afterwards he, being pioneer balloonist, with two others made an ascent from Bath from which he never returned. He was never seen or heard of again.

The following account of the tragedy was given in the *Malmesbury Almanac* of 1883:—

"The late Mr. Walter Powell, Member of Parliament for Malmesbury, 1868 to 1881.

"The lamented death of Mr. Walter Powell, who for fourteen years represented the Borough of Malmesbury in Parliament, is an event the gloom occasioned by which can scarcely yet be said to have passed away.

"Known and loved by the poorest as well as the richest of the constituency, no other feelings than those of the deepest grief filled the minds of all at his sad and untimely fate.

"His great public services to the borough, his constant and unchanging kindness to all in private life, his unbounded benevolence to the sick and suffering poor have gained for him a lasting place in the affection of the people of Malmesbury, in whose hearts his memory must ever live.

"Cast in the midst of an agricultural population whose prosperity was often seriously threatened by adverse seasons, his benevolence found many recipients.

"Moreover, his desire to benefit all classes by the establishment of reading rooms was greatly appreciated sparing as he did no cost to make them popular.

"The melancholy account of his end must be fresh in all our minds, the facts briefly recited are:— On Saturday, December 10th, 1881, Captain Templer, with Mr. Powell and Mr. Agg-Gardner, started from Bath in the balloon Saladin, at mid-day, and crossing over Somerset to Exeter continued their course towards Bridport, and about five o'clock, finding they were rapidly drifting seaward, they attempted to descend.

"The balloon came down with great rapidity and struck the ground with much violence. Mr. Agg-Gardner and Captain Templer were both thrown out of the car, the former gentleman being cut and bruised. Mr. Powell was left in the car and Captain Templer called to him to come down the valve line which he still had hold of, but which was torn out of his hand as he spoke, and the balloon instantly rose to a great height, and drifting rapidly out to sea was soon lost sight of in the darkness. When last seen Mr. Powell was bravely standing up in the car waving an adieu to his comrades.

"Although the most strenuous efforts were made both by the Government and Mr. Powell's relatives to obtain tidings of the balloon, no vestige of it or its occupant was ever afterwards discovered save a thermometer found on the beach and which was identified as belonging to Captain Templer.

"The constituency has yet to perform the duty of perpetuating the memory of its benefactor either by a statutory memorial or a continuance of the excellent institution which did so much towards softening the turmoil inseparable from politics, so that posterity shall not look in vain for a tribute to the memory of so esteemed a philanthropist."

Besides hearing this story from my father I have also heard it from old Charlie Buckland, whose mother, a Miss Goodfield before marriage, was working in Eastcourt House (Mr. Powell's home) at the time. Old Charlie Buckland was one of the first men to volunteer for Active Service at the commencement of World War I in 1914.

He was living at Crudwell at the time and a local farmer drove a horse and wagon from Crudwell to Cirencester Barracks with twenty men from the village who enlisted there and then in the Gloucester Regiment and served throughout the war. Only four of these men returned, among them Charlie Buckland. He was severely wounded, a piece of shrapnel taking part of his mouth and face away. After a long spell in hospital and having about seventeen grafting operations, he was eventually discharged and able to go back to civilian life as a gardener. Except for a few scars remaining and a plate to form the roof of his mouth, no one would imagine what he had been through. Although now nearly eighty years of age, he still rides his bicycle and seldom misses his daily visit to the "local" to enjoy his pint of bitter and a chat.

*   *   *   *

It might be of interest if I gave the following paragraphs from *A Short History of the V.W.H. Earl Bathurst's and Cricklade Hunts* by Daphne Moore.

"The title 'Vale of White Horse' appears somewhat of a misnomer today, when the White Horse, cut out of the chalky hillside near Uffington, lies within the Old Berks. boundaries, but in order to realize the cause of the country being so named it is necessary to turn back this page of history to the year 1830, when the Hon. Henry Moreton (later Lord Ducie) became Master of the Old Berks.

"For some seventy years the Old Berks. had hunted a country whose vast dimensions seem almost incredible to us these days, covering no less than FIVE Hunt countries as constituted at present. Mr. Moreton endeavoured to lighten his well-nigh impossible task of successfully hunting this immense area by conveying hounds to the meet and returning them to kennels after hunting in a van drawn by four post horses, but even so he could not cover the entire country and in 1832 despite considerable opposition, he divided it, taking the western half and moving his kennels from Faringdon to Cricklade.

"He already owned a kennel there for use when hunting the district, but after one season he moved again, this time to Cirencester, where the 4th Earl Bathurst built him new kennels, situated at the east end of his lovely Park. Here appropriately enough, the hounds of the present Earl Bathurst are in kennels today.

"The White Horse of Uffington was included in Mr. Moreton's newly-formed territory, giving the Hunt its name."

"It was in 1886 that the V.W.H. Bathurst Hunt was divided up and V.W.H. (Cirencester) and V.W.H. (Cricklade) came into being."

This arrangement worked satisfactorily for over fifty years. The Hunt suffered a severe blow in 1878 when Major Whyte Melville was tragically killed by a fall on the flat near Braydon Pond.

On the resignation of Lord Shannon as Master after four seasons, Mr. C. A. R.

133

Hoare was appointed to succeed him and after some differences of opinion and misunderstandings it was decided that the Hunt should be split up again, Mr. Hoare taking the Cricklade area where he set up kennels, and thus the V.W.H. (Cricklade) Hunt came into being in the year 1886.

The book *A Short History of the V.W.H.* (*Earl Bathurst's and Cricklade*) *Hunts* by Daphne Moore was written about 1953 or 4, and since that time a further change has taken place, as about ten years later the Hunts were again amalgamated, kennelled at Marston Meysey and known as the V.W.H. It is very significant to note that on Andrews and Dury's map of 1773, there is written across the Minety area "The White Horse" which shows that the district was even then known as the Vale of White Horse.

At the present time there are four Joint Masters: Mr. T. J. Dibble, Mr. M. R. Q. Henriques, Mr. P. G. Hudson and Major J. J. Mann.

*   *   *   *

Royal Observer Corps

HAVING had my share of heroics in the first World War, I was now past military age for call-up. But, previous to the outbreak of war, in 1939, I had joined the "Observer Corps" which was then being formed. The primary object of the Corps was to set up posts over the country to spot, report and track unidentified or hostile aircraft. This meant the members taking the Oath of Allegiance and being sworn in as Special Constables and being issued with a tin hat, a baton or truncheon and a gas mask. After the outbreak we were required to man our posts for twenty-four hours a day, two Observers on duty at a time and usually in four or six-hour shifts. As this was a part-time service we had to work out a rota which suited each member as far as possible.

Before long we were taken over by the Air Ministry. His Majesty King George VI gave his patronage and we were thenceforth named "The Royal Observer Corps." We were then issued with R.A.F.-type blue uniforms and wore the crown above our badge of which we were very proud. Each observation post was connected by telephone to Group Headquarters, ours being at Bristol. Any aircraft was plotted directly it was seen or heard, reported to headquarters who had large table maps marked in squares known as grid references. They in turn passed all information to the Royal Air Force Fighter Command such as identity, whether hostile or friendly, direction of flight, number of aircraft and estimated height. Each post was equipped with a computer instrument mounted on a swivel which was trained on the aircraft being plotted which gave height and direction of flight.

R.O.C. duties had to combine with the running of the farm and milk round whilst also serving on the committee (as village representative) of the National Farmers' Union. I was responsible too for ensuring that in the event of invasion and the Home Guard were mobilised there would be men available to go from farm to farm to milk and feed cows and livestock. This meant visiting every farm and making a census of all men and women who would not be called out and arranging with them which farms they would be responsible for. Fortunately this emergency never arose, but it nevertheless had to be provided for.

Owing to the shortage of petrol, bicycles had to be used as much as possible and I have cycled to Malmesbury on more than one occasion after a full day's work.

It was a common occurrence in the summer months to do two milkings by hand, do haymaking all day, take the tractor and mowing machine and cut grass till after 11 p.m., then have to immobilise the tractor by removing the magneto and hiding it in the hedge in case of enemy airborne invasion (this was compulsory) then change and cycle to the observer post where I would be on duty from midnight until 6 a.m. Then ride home, fetch the cows in for milking with time only for a mouthful of breakfast before starting out on the milk round and another day's work on the farm. After six years of this arduous life we were very near the point of complete exhaustion and could hardly believe our ears when news at last came that the war was over.

This was hastened by the first nuclear weapon being dropped on Hiroshima, with such devastating and disastrous results that it was deemed necessary at once to have some defence here at home. So the primary duty of the "Royal Observer Corps" was changed from spotting hostile aircraft to detecting nuclear fallout. After two years of inactivity following the cessation of hostilities we were to undertake the "Nuclear Defence of Great Britain," being given instruction in the use of instruments for determining the amount of radio activity set up and also the direction of the fallout. This necessitated a great deal of study and took up a lot of time. After having been a member since April 1939, except for the two year stand-down prior to the reorganisation in 1947, I was forced to reluctantly tender my resignation. Age was creeping up on me and I was finding it increasingly difficult to stand up to the hours involved, having the farm to run as well. On doctor's order I had to pull out.

Very fortunately for me, our post, "M.1" in the Oxford Group, had won the challenge trophy for that year as being the most efficient post in the group, which was a stimulus to me in having to make my decision. Better to resign while doing a good job than to go on and possibly be asked to do so on reaching retirement age. I also thought it may give a younger man the chance of promotion. Incidentally, it worked out very well as under the new Chief Observer, Mr. E. J. Price, who succeeded me, the crew went on to win the trophy for the next two years following. As a reward for my contribution and service to the Corps, I had the honour of being granted life membership. I am now entitled to wear the "Royal Observer Corps" badge which indeed makes me feel I still belong, and that I can be identified by any other members or past members I may meet.

Within about a year of handing over my responsibilities in the R.O.C. I had also to give up my farm. My health having taken a turn for the worse, and finding myself unable to cope with it, once again I had to very reluctantly throw in the towel and so bring to a close my varied, though very interesting career, which had included farming, soldiering, garage and motor engineering (with particular emphasis on motor cycles), besides once sampling a short period as foreman in charge of a group of Unemployed Ex-Servicemen after World War I on drainage schemes undertaken by the Wilts. County Council to relieve the unemployment problem.

CHAPTER EIGHT

Conclusion

OF the many incidents I have mentioned in this book and the stories I have told I have made every effort to avoid writing anything at all that may cause any embarrassment to any person young or old who may be tempted to read it. I wanted it to be a book acceptable to any member of the family. I hope that some of my anecdotes, which concern the predecessors or ancestors of so many local families, will be taken as they say in the Latin "Cum Grano Salis" or if I many enlarge upon it "with a liberal sprinkling of salt."

Many stories I have perforce been obliged to leave untold for reasons too numerous and varied to go into. I might just add that were it not for their originality and wit some of them would just as well be forgotten. In any case I am quite content to leave them in their wrappings and perhaps someome else may be inclined to unfold them at some future date.

I very much doubt if anyone achieves every one of his ambitions. But that does not mean that you must give up trying. In about the eighteen-eighties a cousin of my Mother's, Sydney J. Burgoyne, went to America settling in Philadelphia, Pa. Visiting us at Minety in 1927 he told us of a society he had founded named "Friendly Fellows." Every one of the members pledged themselves to the cause of "seeking and finding the Good in Others" and to "live and help live." He accepted my Mother as a member and left with her a copy of his book of poems one of which I will take the risk of including here because it so aptly applies to every one of us.

Winners

Stick to what you've started
 Work for all you're worth
For not to the faint hearted
 Is victory on earth.

The man with faith undaunted
 Who knows his cause is just
Assured of what is wanted
 Fights because he must.

So keep on pitching in
 And make each blow a "hit"
For "Quitters" never win
 And "WINNERS" never quit.

* * * *

Revisiting Swanage

One of my ambitions only fulfilled after more than fifty years was to revisit Swanage, Dorset, for it was there that I spent my training period at the Signal School when I was with the 43rd Reserve Battery, Royal Field Artillery. So in nineteen sixty-eight my wife and I packed a few things in my "Mini," having already booked accommodation in King's Road, which was very central and close to the sea, and set off on a bright sunny day. Every mile was a mile of history.

From the depths of the old Bradon Forest to Malmesbury and there were the ruins of the famous Abbey silhouetted against the skyline on our right. This beautiful old Abbey stripped of much of its former wealth but not of its glory. The landed property of Malmesbury Abbey in the year 1081 included the Manors of HIWEI (in 1808 spelt Hywaye), DANTSIE, SUMERFORD, BRECHEORDE (Brinkworth), NORTONE, BROCHENBERGE (Brokenborough), CHEMELE (Kemble), NEWENTONE (Newnton), CERLETONE (Charlton), GARDONE (Garsdon), CREDVELLE (Crudwell), BREME (Bremhill), PIRITONE (Purton), LITTLETONE (Littleton, Glos.), and NIWE BOLD (Warwicks.).

The area estimated in "Hides" was some two hundred and ninety and at two hundred and thirty hides to the acre this would have brought their estate to some sixty-six thousand, seven hundred acres, bringing in an annual income of £138 10s. It must be remembered that at that time money was worth three times as much as it was in the nineteenth century and perhaps more than twenty times its present value.

But I must press on regardless of Roundheads and Royalists who fought over all this ground.

Taking the Chippenham Road, passing through Melksham, Trowbridge and Westbury, leaving Salisbury and Stonehenge on our left, history seemed to be oozing out all the way round. I began thinking of the Tolpuddle Martyrs who were transported in 1834 for standing up for their rights. No doubt they would have had more success had they not rioted. But tarry not! Away through Shaftesbury and Blandford. Does not the name "Blandford" seem to ring a bell? There was an Earl of Blandford mentioned in the Title Deeds of some of the properties in Bradon Forest. And there is to this day on Swillbrook Farm, Minety, the property of Mr. Peter Hudson, one of the Joint Masters of the V.W.H. Hunt, a piece of pasture described on the schedule as "Late Blandford."

Now here is a matter for someone to straighten out as I am beginning to get a tang of sea air as we continue south towards the old Army Tank training area near Wareham to Corfe Castle about which a volume could be written. As I looked up from the car park below it brought back memories of the days when we were in training, doing signalling schemes, waving flags and flashing lamps from high up on the ramparts trying to make contact with our Brigade on Ballard Down in 1917. Our distant station was the old Obelisk which could be seen for miles around, but alas had to be pulled down during the 39-45 War as it was a landmark for the enemy.

As we approached Swanage passing St. Mary's Church on our right and into King Street, I could seem to hear again the measured tramp of feet and the jingling of spurs swinging along on Church Parade on Sunday mornings, coming to a halt without advancing "Fours left" then breaking step and entering the Church in single file. Those of us who were at the head of the column were seated to the left just inside and so were able to sit and watch the remainder file in, in what seemed an endless line of khaki, bandoliers and spurs. Then before the Service commenced the Clergyman would make an announcement. "Would members of Choirs come up and sit in the Chancel?" There was always a ready response from many of the troops including myself.

But here I am loitering again. There were many things to see including the Old Harry Rocks to the east and Bournemouth. To the west Durlston Head and Castle, the Globe, the Lighthouse and the Old Smugglers' haunt known as the "Tilly Whim Caves." You can almost visualise the boats loaded with contraband discharging their illegal cargoes to be hauled up the cliffs and hidden away in the caves. There was the cargo of matches from a stricken ship which had either been torpedoed or had struck a mine. Thousands of boxes of matches had been washed up along the beach for a mile or two. The troops were soon there with pockets bulging and caps filled with boxes of matches. For weeks the windows of the huts were lined with half open boxes, the heads exposed to allow them to dry out.

Even matches were acceptable, but I think at that time a cargo of salt beef would have been more appreciated.

But enough of this or I shall never finish. I felt I must visit the Church again and have another look round in my own time. The Sunday after arriving at Swanage, my wife and I had walked to the morning service which we much enjoyed. In the afternoon I returned to take one or two snapshots. Hanging in the porch was a framed appeal which so struck me that I made a copy of the text on a leaf of paper and put it in my pocket. Proceeding into the Church after saying a prayer, I heard a slight sound of a cough coming from the Vestry. I walked quietly in that direction where I found that the Vicar was there, the Very Reverend H. D. Anderson, who, up to the time of his retirement to less strenuous activities, had been Bishop of Salisbury and Chaplain to Her Majesty Queen Elizabeth II.

I told him of my association with Swanage and also that I was much impressed by the wording of the appeal in the porch. It ran as follows:—

"The tower of this Church survived the attack of the Danes. The Church survived two world wars, though damaged. It has survived the ravages of time and is our heritage. Will you help towards its survival for future generations?"

He remarked in a quiet voice, "I wrote that," obviously pleased that I had particularly noted it. There must have been many who read and responded to it. We had an interesting conversation and he said that if I would have a word with the Organist and Choirmaster they would fit me up with a cassock and surplice and he would like me to once more sing with the Choir sitting in the same choir stall I had occupied more than fifty years before. That evening I arrived in time to be fitted out with spare robes and took my place with the Bass after being welcomed by the members of the Choir. I could not help feeling honoured when the Vicar, before delivering his sermon from the pulpit said, "We are pleased to welcome back this evening in the Choir, Mr. Manners, who sang here as a lad" and I couldn't help wondering where all the rest of those young men who had filled the Church those many years ago may be. Of all that had happened in the intervening years and of those who had lived and died to make this a better world for everyone.

As I bring this book to a close my final observation must be to quote a saying that comes to mind. "It is not the World but those who live in it. The ultimate decision is theirs."

138